YORK NOTES

D1459386

THE SIGN OF THE FOUR

ARTHUR CONAN DOYLE

NOTES BY JO HEATHCOTE

PEARSON

YORK PRESS

The right of Jo Heathcote to be identified as Author of this Work has
been asserted by her in accordance with the Copyright, Designs and
Patents Act 1988

YORK PRESS
322 Old Brompton Road, London SW5 9JH

PEARSON EDUCATION LIMITED
Edinburgh Gate, Harlow,
Essex CM20 2JE, United Kingdom
Associated companies, branches and representatives throughout the world

© Librairie du Liban *Publishers* 2016

First published 2016

10 9 8 7 6

ISBN 978–1–2921–3813–8

Illustrations by John Rabou; and Alan Batley (page 53 only)

Phototypeset by Swales and Willis Ltd

Printed in Slovakia

Photo credits: Andrii Zezhera/Shutterstock for page 9 / Robcsworld/
Thinkstock for page 11 top / B.erne/Shutterstock for page 11 bottom /
© iStock/Jostaphot for page 13 / © iStock/BeholdingEye for page 15
top / © iStock/PhotoVic for page 15 bottom / Igor Chernomorchenko/
Shutterstock for page 17 / © iStock/Daniya Melnikova for page 19 / ©
iStock/Studiocasper for page 20 / FPWing/Shutterstock for page 22 /
©iStock/Katpaws for page 23 / © iStock/Nsj-images for page 25 / ©
iStock/719production for page 26 / © iStock/ImPerfectLazyBones for page
27 / Michaela Stejskalova/Shutterstock for page 30 / Ingram Publishing/
Thinkstock for page 33 / Alvaro Puig/Shutterstock for page 43 / © iStock/
Cristian Baitg for page 44 / Gunnar Pippel/Shutterstock for page 46 /
Delicate/Shutterstock for page 48 / Olga Popova/Shutterstock for page
49 / PHOTOS.COM/Thinkstock for page 50 top / Alexander Mazurkevich/
Shutterstock for page 50 bottom / Vorobyeva/Shutterstock for page 51 /
© iStock/ericsphotography for page 52 / homydesign/Shutterstock for page
55 / Luisa Fumi/Shutterstock for page 56 / Fenton one/Shutterstock for page
57 / Jaroslaw Grudzinski/Shutterstock for page 58 / © iStock/ValEs1989 for
page 59 / moomsabuy/Shutterstock for page 60 / © iStock/Steve Debenport
for page 71 / wavebreakmedia/Shutterstock for page 73

CONTENTS

PART FOUR:
THEMES, CONTEXTS AND SETTINGS

PART FIVE:
FORM, STRUCTURE AND LANGUAGE

PART SIX:
PROGRESS BOOSTER ★

PART SEVEN:
FURTHER STUDY AND ANSWERS

PART ONE: GETTING STARTED

PREPARING FOR ASSESSMENT

HOW WILL I BE ASSESSED ON MY WORK ON *THE SIGN OF THE FOUR*?

The Sign of the Four is set by AQA only and your work will be examined through these three Assessment Objectives:

Assessment Objectives	Wording	Worth thinking about ...
A01	Read, understand and respond to texts. Students should be able to: ● maintain a critical style and develop an informed personal response ● use textual references, including quotations, to support and illustrate interpretations.	● How well do I know what happens, what people say, do, etc.? ● What do *I* think about the key ideas in the novella? ● How can I support my viewpoint in a really convincing way? ● What are the best quotations to use and when should I use them?
A02	Analyse the language, form and structure used by a writer to create meanings and effects, using relevant subject terminology where appropriate.	● What specific things does the writer 'do'? What choices has Conan Doyle made (why this particular word, phrase or paragraph here? Why does this event happen at this point?) ● What effects do these choices create – suspense? mystery? humour?
A03	Show understanding of the relationships between texts and the contexts in which they were written.	● What can I learn about society from the novella? (What does it tell me about justice and prejudice, for example?) ● What was society like in Conan Doyle's time? Can I see it reflected in the text?

Look out for the Assessment Objective labels throughout your York Notes Study Guide – these will help to focus your study and revision!

The text used in this Study Guide is the Collins Classic edition, 2015.

HOW TO USE YOUR YORK NOTES STUDY GUIDE

You are probably wondering what is the best and most efficient way to use your York Notes Study Guide on *The Sign of the Four.* Here are three possibilities:

A step-by-step study and revision guide	A 'dip-in' support when you need it	A revision guide after you have finished the text
Step 1: Read Part Two as you read the novella, as a companion to help you study it. **Step 2:** When you need to, flip forward to Parts Three to Five to focus your learning. **Step 3**: Then, when you have finished, use Parts Six and Seven to hone your exam skills, revise and practise for the exam.	Perhaps you know the text quite well, but you want to check your understanding and practise your exam skills? Just look for the section you think you need most help with and go for it!	You might want to use the Notes after you have finished your study, using Parts Two to Five to check over what you have learned, and then work through Parts Six and Seven in the immediate weeks leading up to your exam.

HOW WILL THE GUIDE HELP YOU STUDY AND REVISE?

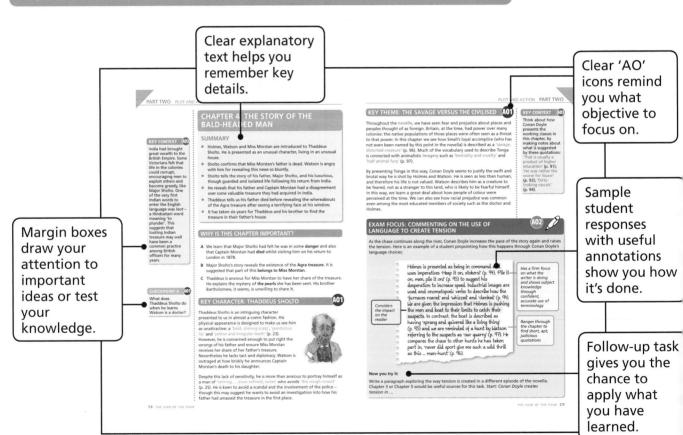

Clear explanatory text helps you remember key details.

Clear 'AO' icons remind you what objective to focus on.

Margin boxes draw your attention to important ideas or test your knowledge.

Sample student responses with useful annotations show you how it's done.

Follow-up task gives you the chance to apply what you have learned.

Extra references help you focus your revision.

Themes are explained clearly with bullet-points which give you ideas you might use in your essay responses.

This section helps you tackle or explore challenging ideas or gives you a deeper insight into the writer's methods.

This section introduces an important quotation, explains what it means and shows its effects.

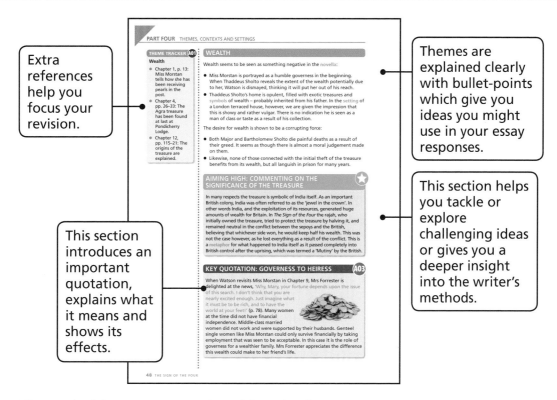

Parts **Two** to **Five** end with a **Progress and Revision check**:

A set of quick questions tests your knowledge of the text.

Further substantial and 'open' tasks test your understanding.

Self-evaluation helps you keep a record of how you are getting on.

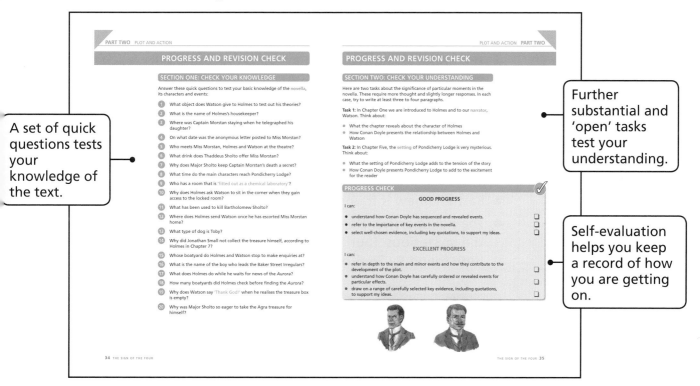

Don't forget **Parts Six** and **Seven**, with advice and practice on **improving your writing skills**:

- Focus on **difficult areas** such as **'context'** and **'inferences'**
  - **Short snippets** of **other students' work** to show you how it's done (or not done!)
  - Three annotated **sample responses** to a task **at different levels**, with **expert comments**, to help you judge your own level
- **Practice questions**
  - **Answers** to the **Progress and Revision Checks** and **Checkpoint** margin boxes

Now it's up to you! Don't forget – there's even more help on our website with more sample answers, essay planners and even online tutorials. Go to www.yorknotes.com to find out more.

PLOT SUMMARY

CHAPTERS 1–2: DAY 1, AFTERNOON

- The characters of Holmes and Watson are introduced. Holmes is bored and is taking cocaine to replace the mental activity he craves. Watson is disapproving.
- Miss Morstan arrives, having been recommended Holmes's detective services. She tells him of her case. Her father disappeared some years previously on his return from military service in India. She has been sent a valuable pearl each year for the past six years and has now received an anonymous letter requesting a meeting.
- Holmes is immediately alert and ready for action.

CHAPTERS 3–6: DAY 1, EVENING/NIGHT

- Holmes completes some initial research. Holmes, Miss Morstan and Watson go to a mysterious meeting at the Lyceum Theatre. They are met by a coachman and escorted to Thaddeus Sholto's home in the London suburbs.
- The house is unusual and the connection with India is established. Sholto tells them that his father, Major Sholto, is dead. The Major was a friend of Miss Morstan's father, who he says is also dead. It is revealed that Major Sholto had some Indian treasure – part of which seemed to belong to Captain Morstan.
- The action moves to Pondicherry Lodge, home of the late Major Sholto and Thaddeus's twin brother, Bartholomew.
- Bartholomew is found murdered and the treasure stolen.
- The police arrive. Holmes names his suspect as Jonathan Small, one of the mysterious 'four' mentioned in Captain Mortsan's papers and on the note found by Sholto's body.

CHAPTER 7–8: DAY 2, EARLY HOURS OF THE MORNING

- After an initial investigation by the police inspector Athelney Jones, Thaddeus Sholto and the staff of Pondicherry Lodge are arrested.
- Watson takes Miss Morstan back to her home at Mrs Cecil Forrester's.
- Holmes instructs Watson to collect a dog, Toby, from a contact he has in Lambeth. Watson returns to Pondicherry Lodge with the dog, to find Holmes gathering more clues.
- A tiny bare footprint found in the attic above Sholto's room suggests Small had an unusual accomplice.
- Toby traces the scent of creosote from Sholto's room. Though the search initially draws a blank, it finally leads them to the River Thames.

CHAPTER 8: DAY 2, MORNING

- Holmes discovers Mordecai Smith's boatyard and gathers information from his wife and son about their boat, the *Aurora*. Holmes believes the real suspects have hired the boat and Smith's services.
- Holmes and Watson return to Baker Street and eat breakfast. They read the newspaper accounts of the crime.
- The Baker Street Irregulars search for Smith's boat.
- Watson sleeps.

CHAPTER 9: DAY 2, LATE AFTERNOON/EVENING

- Watson returns Toby to his owner and visits Miss Morstan.
- On his return, he finds Mrs Hudson to be worried about Holmes, who is pacing his room, having had no sleep.

CHAPTER 9: DAY 3–4

- Holmes still hasn't slept and passes the day in a dejected mood because there is still no word of the *Aurora*.
- Disguised as a sailor, he leaves Baker Street to search for the *Aurora*.
- Watson sees the advertisement Holmes has placed in the newspaper offering a reward for information.
- Athelney Jones arrives. Holmes has summoned him via telegram. He confesses to Watson that he needs help with the case.
- Holmes returns disguised as an old sailor and fools Watson and Jones. He has made progress with the case. He asks Jones to help with a police boat and back-up that evening.

CHAPTERS 10–12: DAY 4, EVENING/NIGHT

- Watson, Holmes and Jones have dinner before heading for the river.
- The *Aurora* leaves the boat repairers where it was hidden. Following Holmes's orders, the police launch follows it at speed.
- Tonga, Small's accomplice, is shot and killed. Jonathan Small is captured and confesses to Holmes.
- Watson takes the treasure box to Miss Morstan's where it is found to be empty. Watson declares his love to Miss Morstan.
- Back at Baker Street, Small tells Holmes, Watson and Jones how the Agra treasure came to be in Major Sholto's possession. Jones takes Small into custody, leaving Holmes and Watson together.

REVISION FOCUS: STORIES WITHIN THE STORY

Though Watson narrates the main plot chronologically, there are many other stories throughout the novella, which shed a light on the case. List all the characters who tell their story to Holmes and Watson and summarise the clues that each story gives to both Holmes and the reader.

KEY CONTEXT (A03)

221b Baker Street is the place that is most closely connected with Sherlock Holmes stories. However, Conan Doyle makes use of a number of different and important locations throughout the novella. List all of the London locations that are visited as the story develops. What is the significance of each location? For example: the Lyceum Theatre – where Miss Morstan is asked to wait in the anonymous letter.

CHAPTER 1: THE SCIENCE OF DEDUCTION

SUMMARY

- Doctor Watson expresses his concern for Sherlock Holmes as he watches him inject a cocaine solution into his arm.
- Sherlock Holmes talks of his profession as a detective and his need to be constantly stimulated by his work.
- Holmes tells Watson that he has been advising a French detective, as well as writing specialist reference books on the scientific aspects of detection.
- Watson tests Holmes's skills by giving him a pocket watch to examine and comment on.
- Holmes admits he is bored without a case to work on and says this explains his use of drugs.
- The housekeeper, Mrs Hudson, brings news of a visitor, Miss Morstan.

WHY IS THIS CHAPTER IMPORTANT?

A We are introduced to both **Holmes** and the framework narrator **Watson**.

B We learn that Holmes has **invented** his own **profession** as a **consulting detective** and that he has a reputation as a **genius** in his field.

C We learn that Watson has been injured in battle, is a **doctor** and is concerned for Holmes's well-being.

TOP TIP (A02)

When Watson exclaims to Holmes, 'You really are an automaton,–a calculating machine' (p. 15), he is contrasting Holmes's way of looking at life with his own. This metaphor suggests Holmes is without emotion and perhaps rather insensitive. However, at other points in the novella, we do see a more sensitive side to Holmes – he is reassuring to Thaddeus Sholto that he will clear him of criminal charges, he is kind to protect Jones's professional reputation and he is civil and thoughtful towards Jonathan Small after his capture.

KEY CONTEXT: VICTORIAN ATTITUDES TO DRUG USE

During Victorian times, many of the drugs that are now classed as highly dangerous and addictive were sold in chemist shops. Different drugs were brought to Britain from the British Empire. Their dangers and addictive nature were not yet known or widely researched. Using drugs recreationally was popular with many writers and artists of the nineteenth century, for example Coleridge, Lord Byron, Shelley and Keats. They believed using substances such as opium and cocaine enhanced their creative abilities. Here, Sherlock Holmes seems to believe the drug helps him to be more perceptive and mentally alert.

AIMING HIGH: COMMENTING ON THE NARRATIVE VOICE

Watson is a major character in the novella, but it is important to consider his role as narrator too. It is Watson's thoughts, perceptions and views that we are presented with. Watson is speaking as a 'medical man' (p. 2) and clearly disapproves of Holmes's drug use. He is also worried that he may offend Holmes if he offers him advice or challenges him. He praises Holmes's 'extraordinary genius for minutiae [i.e. detail]' (p. 5) and seems fascinated by Holmes's cases. Watson says he has written up a previous case and named it 'A Study in Scarlet' (p. 3). This adds to the realistic nature of Watson as narrator as this is a published Sherlock Holmes story.

However, Watson is also somewhat sceptical and disbelieving of Holmes and wishes to put his 'theories to a more severe test' (p. 6). He questions Holmes's ideas and methods in the same way that a reader might. In this way Conan Doyle is able to make Holmes appear convincing.

KEY QUOTATION: AN ACTIVE MIND

Holmes offers an insight into why he is presented as a genius in his field when he states, 'I cannot live without brain-work' (p. 9). It suggests he is a man of great intellectual ability, who can be fulfilled only by stimulating, active problem-solving. It seems that using his abilities is less a passion or an obsession, than a basic need for Holmes.

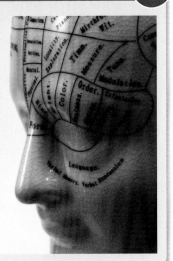

TOP TIP A01

Watson shows that he has mixed feelings about Holmes in this first chapter. Make a list of the key quotations that show Watson's range of feelings for Holmes. Make notes on your findings about the character of Holmes from those quotations.

CHECKPOINT 1 A01

Sherlock Holmes seems unimpressed with the work of three other professional detectives in this opening chapter. What are their names?

CHAPTER 2: THE STATEMENT OF THE CASE

SUMMARY

- The character of Miss Morstan is introduced. She explains how her employer has recommended Holmes to her.
- She tells Holmes and Watson of the mysterious disappearance of her father ten years previously. He had just come home to London on leave from an army post in India.
- She adds to the mystery by explaining how she was tracked down through a newspaper advertisement four years later. She has been sent a valuable pearl, anonymously, once a year ever since.
- Miss Morstan shows Holmes a letter requesting a meeting with her in a public place, outside a theatre, that evening. She is allowed to bring two friends for safety, but not the police.
- Holmes is stimulated by the challenge of the case. He immediately begins to look for clues within the letter and the handwriting.
- Watson is distracted by the looks and character of Miss Morstan and begins to entertain romantic thoughts of her.

WHY IS THIS CHAPTER IMPORTANT?

A   The beginnings of a **mysterious case** are presented to Holmes through Miss Morstan's **visit** and **story**.

B   The letter's suggestion that 'two friends' (p. 14) should accompany **Miss Morstan** allows Watson to be part of the investigation.

C   The different reactions of Holmes and Watson to Miss Morstan mean that two contrasting themes begin to emerge: **scientific deduction** and **romance**.

KEY CHARACTER: MISS MORSTAN   (A01)

Miss Morstan is presented to us through the eyes of Watson and his judgements on her are almost certainly designed to show his immediate attraction to her. He describes her outward appearance in detail, observing that Miss Morstan cannot be rich as she appears to be 'of limited means' (p. 11), but she has 'the most perfect taste' (p. 11). Miss Morstan is portrayed as being vulnerable and a victim, in need of help and protection. Even the mysterious letter describes her as 'a wronged woman' (p. 14). She is presented as a classic Victorian stereotype of perfect womanhood: passive, gentle and in need of male protection.

TOP TIP   (A01)

The letter Miss Morstan receives asking her to meet at the theatre that evening is dated 7 July. Construct a timeline working back through her story to her childhood. Add notes onto it outlining the major events of her case.

Holmes describes her as a 'model client' (p. 14) as a result of her composed and organised account and the fact she has brought all the documents for the case. Watson, on the other hand, can only think 'dangerous thoughts' (p. 16) as he reflects on meeting Miss Morstan that afternoon. As Watson thinks of her 'smiles' (p. 16) and her 'refined and sensitive nature' (p. 11), Conan Doyle is setting the scene for future romance.

KEY QUOTATION: A CASE FOR HOLMES (A01)

In contrast to Holmes's earlier restlessness Miss Morstan's visit brings about a change in Holmes. 'Holmes rubbed his hands, and his eyes glistened. He leaned forward in his chair with an expression of extraordinary concentration upon his clear-cut, hawk-like features' (p.12). His earlier comments about his need for stimulation in work are matched by his physical actions, which show his barely concealed excitement at the prospect of a case to solve. Everything about Holmes now seems sharp, not just his mental capacity but the actual look and shape of his face, described like an agile and focused bird of prey.

TOP TIP: WRITING ABOUT SMALL DETAILS (A02)

In Chapter 1, Watson observes that Holmes has a gift for observing small details. In this chapter, you could observe and record the small details that Conan Doyle presents us with in order to keep track of developments later on.

Make some careful notes of the names, dates and places in the chapter. They offer a number of contextual clues worth exploring. The references to 'Indian regiment' (p. 12), 'the 'Andaman Islands', 'a very large and lustrous pearl' (p. 13) add an exotic quality to the text. India was an important and valuable British colony at the time the novella is set. How might this add a different dimension to the story than its London setting? How might this capture your imagination?

CHECKPOINT 2 (A02)

What reasons does Watson give for believing he is unworthy of Miss Morstan once he realises he is attracted to her?

CHAPTER 3: IN QUEST OF A SOLUTION

SUMMARY

- Holmes has spent the afternoon investigating the case. He makes a connection between the date of Major Sholto's death and Miss Morstan receiving the first of the pearls.
- Miss Morstan arrives in a carriage. Holmes and Watson join her to go to the Lyceum Theatre. Holmes takes a revolver and Watson a heavy walking cane.
- Miss Morstan introduces a new clue: a drawing or plan of a building marked with 'The sign of the four' and the names of four men.
- A coachman meets Holmes, Watson and Miss Morstan outside the Lyceum Theatre. They are driven out of the crowds in central London to the suburbs.
- They are surprised to find the door of an ordinary suburban terraced house opened by an Indian servant in traditional clothes.

TOP TIP (A02)

Look for contrasting images or ideas in the chapters as you read them and keep track of them. In this chapter think about the contrast between Holmes and Watson; the ordinary people of London and the rich theatre-goers; and the suburban house and the Indian servant. Consider how these contrasts add depth, interest and intrigue to Conan Doyle's plot.

WHY IS THIS CHAPTER IMPORTANT?

A Holmes connects **Major Sholto's heir** to the case, suggesting he must know something of the gifts of the **pearls**.

B The **drawing** with its red cross adds a **complication** and a further dimension to the mystery as well as introducing the **names of more characters** into the **plot**.

C We are taken on a journey through **London**. The figure of Sholto's **Indian servant** adds to the sense of **intrigue** and **mystery** unfolding.

KEY LANGUAGE: THE DESCRIPTION OF LONDON (A02)

Conan Doyle uses the setting of London to add mystery and tension. He paints a stereotypical Victorian image of the city at night, shrouded in 'dense drizzly fog' with lamps casting 'misty splotches of diffused light' (p. 19). Conan Doyle uses pathetic fallacy here to create an atmosphere that has an impact on all three of the characters. Watson is feeling 'nervous and depressed' as is Miss Morstan (p. 20). The streets of London are described as being obscured, lacking in light and clarity – rather like the mystery itself at this point.

Holmes's thoughts, which he must 'reconsider' (p. 19) through the journey, seem also to have receded 'back into the gloom' (p. 20) as he thinks about the drawing. Conan Doyle moves the characters 'at a furious pace through the foggy streets' (p. 20). Holmes maps the journey for us by naming the streets and squares as they pass through. The city is described as a growing, living creature with a sense of threat through the metaphor of 'monster tentacles' (p. 22). This is confirmed by Watson's judgement of the area as being 'questionable' and 'forbidding' (p. 21).

REVISION FOCUS: EXAMINING THE CLUES

Miss Morstan says of the drawing, which she has found among her father's papers, 'I don't suppose that it is of the slightest importance' (p. 18). However, four phrases are used to describe Holmes on page 19, which indicate that the drawing may be of great importance to him: 'drawn brow', 'vacant eye', 'thinking intently' and 'impenetrable reserve'. Look carefully at the information on the plan and the description of Holmes. Make notes on what questions the drawing raises for both Holmes and the reader at this point.

CHECKPOINT 3 (A01)

Identify two quotations in this chapter that indicate Watson's growing admiration for Miss Morstan.

CHAPTER 4: THE STORY OF THE BALD-HEADED MAN

SUMMARY

- Holmes, Watson and Miss Morstan are introduced to Thaddeus Sholto. He is presented as an unusual character, living in an unusual house.
- Sholto confirms that Miss Morstan's father is dead. Watson is angry with him for revealing this news so bluntly.
- Sholto tells the story of his father, Major Sholto, and his luxurious, though guarded and isolated life following his return from India.
- He reveals that his father and Captain Morstan had a disagreement over some valuable treasure they had acquired in India.
- Thaddeus tells us his father died before revealing the whereabouts of the Agra treasure after seeing a terrifying face at his window.
- It has taken six years for Thaddeus and his brother to find the treasure in their father's house.

WHY IS THIS CHAPTER IMPORTANT?

A We learn that Major Sholto had felt he was in some **danger** and also that Captain Morstan had **died** whilst visiting him on his return to London in 1878.

B Major Sholto's story reveals the existence of the **Agra treasure**. It is suggested that part of this **belongs to Miss Morstan**.

C Thaddeus is anxious for Miss Morstan to have her share of the treasure. He explains the mystery of **the pearls** she has been sent. His brother Bartholomew, it seems, is unwilling to share it.

KEY CHARACTER: THADDEUS SHOLTO

Thaddeus Sholto is an intriguing character presented to us in almost a comic fashion. His physical appearance is designed to make us see him as unattractive: a 'bald, shining scalp', 'pendulous lip' and 'yellow and irregular teeth' (p. 23). However, he is concerned enough to put right the wrongs of his father and ensure Miss Morstan receives her share of her father's treasure. Nevertheless he lacks tact and diplomacy. Watson is outraged at how briskly he announces Captain Morstan's death to his daughter.

Despite this lack of sensitivity, he is more than anxious to portray himself as a man of 'retiring, ... even refined, tastes' who avoids 'the rough crowd' (p. 25). He is keen to avoid a scandal and the involvement of the police – though this may suggest he wants to avoid an investigation into how his father had amassed the treasure in the first place.

EXAM FOCUS: COMMENTING ON CONAN DOYLE'S DESCRIPTION

Think about how Conan Doyle adds to the sense of a character by describing their surroundings. Read this example of a student commenting on Thaddeus Sholto's room:

> Despite being in the London suburbs, Sholto's room is presented as palatial with its 'richest' tapestries, 'Oriental' vases and 'Two great tiger-skins'. It seems as though India and its culture has had an impact not just on Sholto's father but on Thaddeus Sholto too. He lives like a maharajah, or Indian prince, with his 'Hindoo servant'.
>
> There is a sense of Sholto seeking to elevate his own social status to that of a gentleman or officer in the colonies. He seems to see this lifestyle as desirable and romantic, smoking with a 'hookah', and displaying his tiger skins, not considering the exploitation that took place through the colonisation of a vast country like India.

Uses precise textual details as evidence

Makes a perceptive inference linked to contextual ideas

Demonstrates knowledge of historical context

Now you try it:

Choose a different room described in the novella and write a paragraph about what it implies about its owner. Start: *Conan Doyle creates a more developed picture of the character of …*

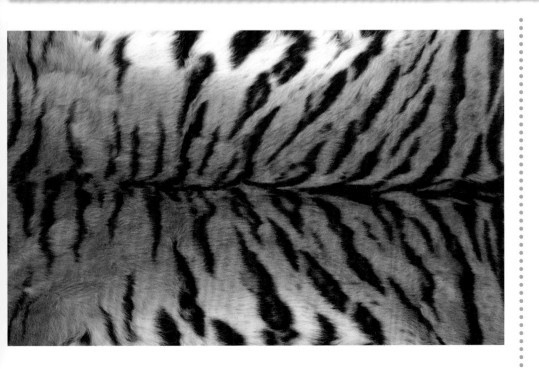

CHAPTER 5: THE TRAGEDY OF PONDICHERRY LODGE

SUMMARY

- Holmes, Watson and Miss Morstan accompany Thaddeus Sholto to Pondicherry Lodge late at night.
- They have trouble being admitted until Holmes reveals who he is to the gatekeeper.
- The house is in darkness and the housekeeper is clearly frightened.
- Bartholomew Sholto, Thaddeus's twin, is locked in his room.
- Holmes and Watson break into the room and find Bartholomew has been murdered with a poisoned thorn. The treasure is missing.
- Holmes sends Thaddeus Sholto to fetch the police, leaving him free to investigate the crime scene.

WHY IS THIS CHAPTER IMPORTANT?

A We move to the Sholto home where the **treasure** has been hidden.

B We **discover** a second member of the **Sholto family** to be **dead** – possibly as a result of the treasure.

C It becomes clear that Miss Morstan is **attracted** to Watson and turns to him for **support**.

CHECKPOINT 5 A01

What are the names of Bartholomew Sholto's servants and how does one of them know and recognise Holmes?

KEY FORM: GOTHIC HORROR

Despite its pleasant sounding name, Pondicherry Lodge is shrouded in mystery. Conan Doyle presents us with all the elements we might expect from the Gothic horror tradition. For example, the company arrive late at night; there is only 'half a moon'; the lodge is isolated within its 'very high stone wall' and behind an 'iron clamped door' (p. 34). There is a sense of entering a castle in a horror story as McMurdo opens the gate with a 'clanking and jarring of keys' (p. 34). Conan Doyle uses noun phrases such as 'desolate grounds' and 'deathly silence' (p. 36) to develop the Gothic feel. However, we know the company have arrived by coach and are still in the London suburbs of Upper Norwood. The fact that Bartholomew's room is set up like a laboratory is never explained, but it adds to the Gothic convention. It might remind readers of famous Gothic settings such as Frankenstein's laboratory.

AIMING HIGH: COMMENTING ON CONAN DOYLE'S DEVELOPMENT OF THE PLOT

Holmes seems almost arrogant in this chapter when he declares that 'I only require a few missing links to have an entirely connected case' (p. 41). However, Conan Doyle has structured this chapter to allow us to unravel the mystery with Holmes. It is worth thinking about the locked room, and about the method by which Bartholomew has been murdered. The implications of the 'long, dark thorn' (p. 41), presumably poisoned, imply a foreign influence. The fact that the treasure is connected to the colony of India leads us to see its connection with ill-fated events, fear, threat and death.

TOP TIP

Make some notes on how men and women are presented differently in this chapter. For example, what behaviours do the women show compared to the men? What does this tell you about how the different genders were viewed at the time Conan Doyle was writing?

KEY QUOTATION: PROTECTING MISS MORSTAN

In contrast to the darkness and death of Chapter 5, we are presented with the childlike innocence of Watson's and Miss Morstan's developing love, 'we stood hand in hand like two children and there was peace in our hearts for all the dark things that surrounded us' (p. 37).

In Chapter 4, Thaddeus Sholto reveals the expected value of the treasure. This would make Miss Morstan a wealthy woman. Watson is troubled by this and fears that her changed status would make a love relationship impossible because of their different social classes. Now Conan Doyle presents their relationship as a healthy contrast to the events at the Lodge. It perhaps gives the reader a moral lesson that this 'most natural thing' (p. 37) is preferable to the greed, suspicious dealings and affectations of the Sholto household with its dubious and possibly ill-gotten treasures.

CHAPTER 6: SHERLOCK HOLMES GIVES A DEMONSTRATION

SUMMARY

- Holmes investigates the scene of the murder and points out clues for the benefit of both Watson and the reader.
- They establish that a man with a wooden leg was involved in the crime and needed an accomplice to help him get into the room.
- Holmes encourages Watson to conclude that the suspect used the roof. They investigate the attic space, where a small bare footprint is found.
- Their investigation is interrupted by the arrival of the police inspector Athelney Jones.
- Jones speculates on the crime and seems content to blame Thaddeus Sholto for his brother's death.
- Holmes, keen to prove Jones wrong, names Jonathan Small as the suspect
- Holmes despatches Watson to take Miss Morstan home and collect a dog, Toby, to help them track down Small and the accomplice Holmes believes is involved.

TOP TIP (A01)

Make a list of all of the clues that Sherlock Holmes and Watson detect at the crime scene. Then make a list of all of the assumptions that Athelney Jones makes which are later proved to be mistakes. What is Conan Doyle implying about Holmes and his methods? What might he be suggesting about the police methods at the time?

TOP TIP (A01)

Think about how Holmes acts almost like a dog following the scent of each clue and taking a new path each time a dead end is reached (p. 45). On page 46, Watson considers Holmes to be like a 'bloodhound' as he examines the clues at Pondicherry Lodge.

WHY IS THIS CHAPTER IMPORTANT?

A We **investigate** the **crime scene** with Holmes and Watson and consider the **clues**.

B Sherlock Holmes's **scientific approach** to detective work is contrasted with the **assumptions** made by the **police inspector**.

C We begin to see the **connections** with the name **Jonathan Small** on Miss Morstan's drawing.

KEY SETTING: THE LOCKED ROOM (A01)

In any detective story, the description of the scene of the crime is a pivotal moment. Conan Doyle presents the scene through Watson's eyes. In this way, we investigate it with him and piece together the clues from Sherlock Holmes's observations, questions and rather impatient prompts. The mystery of the locked door is, of course, the first obstacle to overcome as Holmes questions Watson, 'how did these folk come, and how did they go?' (p. 43). The window allows Conan Doyle to bring back the idea of the one-legged man – reminding us of the fears of Major Sholto himself. Rather conveniently, Holmes finds a lengthy piece of rope and a 'great hook in the wall' (p. 44).

The secret room above, with its trap door to the roof, provides Conan Doyle with the means to bring Jonathan Small's accomplice into the story. In the dust are found, 'the prints of a naked foot' (p. 46). Again, rather conveniently, the crime scene contains the broken container of creosote – though why Sholto had this item in his laboratory is never explained. It is a clearly a **device** included by the author to enable the suspect to be tracked as he 'had the misfortune to tread in the creosote' (p. 47).

REVISION FOCUS: EXPLORING CHARACTER THROUGH LANGUAGE

Look at the contrasting language in the table below used to present Sherlock Holmes and Athelney Jones in this chapter. Write a paragraph about each character, exploring the impression that Conan Doyle creates of them. How do you think Holmes and Jones feel about each other?

Holmes	Jones
'his beady eyes gleaming' (p. 46)	'heavy steps' (p. 47)
'like those of a trained blood-hound picking out a scent' (p. 46)	'loud crash' (p. 47)
	'red-faced, burly and plethoric' (p. 48)
'the dead man very considerately got up and locked the door on the inside' (p. 49)	'It's Mr. Sherlock Holmes, the theorist.' (p. 48)
'He [Jones] has occasional glimmerings of reason' (p. 50)	'said the fat detective, pompously' (p. 49)
'I shall study the great Jones's methods and listen to his not too delicate sarcasms' (p. 52)	'some hocus-pocus' (p. 50)
	'"the other man–?" said Athelney Jones, in a sneering voice' (p. 51)

KEY CONTEXT A03

The scene of the crime and the brief moment before the police arrive allows Conan Doyle to give us more detail about the poisoned dart and the idea that it was not 'an English thorn' (p. 48). This would add tension for Victorian readers as they contemplate the dangerous influence of the outside world. It may suggest that something 'other' than what they are familiar and comfortable with may be at the heart of the crime.

CHAPTER 7: THE EPISODE OF THE BARREL

SUMMARY

- Watson escorts Miss Morstan home to Mrs Forrester's house.
- He continues on to Pinchin Lane where he wakes up Mr Sherman to collect Toby the dog.
- Back at Pondicherry Lodge, Athelney Jones has arrested the entire household.
- Holmes climbs onto the roof to work out how Small's accomplice entered and left the property. He finds a pouch of poisoned darts.
- Holmes gives Toby the scent of the creosote to follow.
- Holmes and Watson are led across London by Toby.
- Toby leads them to a barrel of creosote and not to the suspects.

TOP TIP (A01)

Make a list of all the characters that know Holmes by his reputation. Find one quotation for each character that explains how they think of Sherlock Holmes. For example:
Mrs Forrester – 'She was much impressed by your kindness and skill' (p. 11).

WHY IS THIS CHAPTER IMPORTANT?

A The **romantic theme** of Watson's affection for Miss Morstan is developed.

B Athelney Jones's **arrests** mean the house is empty for Holmes to **investigate further**.

C The **expedition** across **London** allows Conan Doyle to **recap** on the plot and **summarise** the clues.

KEY CHARACTER: SHERLOCK HOLMES (A01)

We have been constantly reminded of Holmes's reputation throughout the novella, and Holmes's name seems to allow the investigators free access to anywhere in London. Watson considers the case, 'a labyrinth in which a man less singularly endowed than my fellow-lodger might well despair of ever finding the clue' (p. 55). This raises Holmes's status above the commonplace in terms of his ability to think strategically and logically.

The contrast is made between Holmes and the regular police force. Whilst Jones has been arresting everyone in sight, Holmes is standing 'with his hands in his pockets, smoking his pipe' (p. 56), relaxed, confident and assured that he has solved the case. He displays his confident athleticism by scaling the roof, 'It was easy to follow him' (p. 58). Despite the fact he is in a 'most break-neck place' (p. 58) and carrying a lantern he also manages to pick up the pouch of poisoned thorns.

Holmes can, however, be insufferable and patronises Watson, 'Pshaw, my dear boy! It was simplicity itself' (p. 60), 'Do you follow all this?' (p. 62).

Though Holmes is much more analytical than Jones, he too is capable of making assumptions about things he cannot possibly know unless he has witnessed them: 'In a frenzy lest the secret of the treasure die with him ... Mad with hate' (p. 61). The humour of this is established when his idea of using Toby comes to an **anticlimactic** end in the timber yard. Even Holmes laughs at his own mistake in following Toby on a false trail.

CHECKPOINT 6 (A01)

Which places in London do Holmes and Watson pass through with Toby in this chapter? You could check on a map to see which of them still remain and how far the two investigators must have walked.

EXAM FOCUS: ENGLISHNESS AND FOREIGNNESS   (A03)

Read this example of a student considering the importance of historical context in the novella:

> Conan Doyle shows us how society at this time could be very narrow-minded and mistrustful of foreign influences. So far, everything connected with India, the Andaman Islands and the Agra treasure has been viewed negatively - even down to the decorations in Thaddeus Sholto's home. On taking Miss Morstan home, Watson observes, 'It was soothing to catch even that passing glimpse of a tranquil English home in the midst of the wild, dark business which had absorbed us' (p. 54), suggesting that Conan Doyle's readership may have believed that England was the best example of civilised life and all that was right.

Makes good use of textual details from earlier in the novella

Uses social context in a subtle way

Now you try it:

Select another quotation from Chapter 7 that deals with gender, race or social class. Write a paragraph exploring what this might tell us about attitudes at the time of writing. Start: *When Conan Doyle was writing 'The Sign of the Four' ...*

CHAPTER 8: THE BAKER STREET IRREGULARS

SUMMARY

- Holmes and Watson retrace their steps and Toby leads them to the river.
- Holmes deduces that the suspects have hired a boat from Mordecai Smith's boatyard. He receives information from Smith's wife confirming that her husband has set sail, with the one-legged man, on his steam launch (a river boat running on a steam-powered engine).
- Holmes and Watson return to Baker Street, stopping only to send a telegram to the Baker Street Irregulars.
- They have breakfast and read the newspaper account of Jones's arrests.
- The doorbell rings and they are visited by the Baker Street Irregulars, a group of street urchins, who are paid by Holmes to go in search of the steam launch.

CHECKPOINT 7

Note down all of the information Holmes gathers about the steam launch from Mrs Smith.

WHY IS THIS CHAPTER IMPORTANT?

A The **chase** of the suspects takes a fresh and **dramatic turn**.

B We witness more of **Holmes's intriguing methods** of investigation.

C We are given more details and clues about **Jonathan Small's accomplice**.

KEY LANGUAGE: THE 'OTHER' MAN (A02)

Jonathan Small's accomplice has been described up to now as 'other'. Conan Doyle has presented him as being a mystery figure. This is a reflection of the Gothic element of the novella, where the unknown character is one to be feared, rather like Bram Stoker's *Dracula* or the creature in Mary Shelley's *Frankenstein*. Here, Holmes describes him as 'absolutely unique', and Watson brands him 'A savage!' (p. 74) – someone who is uncivilised, untamed and outside of society. We are presented with what seems to be a factual description from Holmes's reference book. However, the language from this text is also filled with negative stereotypes of the Andaman aborigines with adjectives such as 'fierce, morose' and noun phrases such as 'naturally hideous'. The brutality of this race of people is emphasised, 'a terror', 'braining their survivors', 'poisoned arrows', 'cannibal feast' (p. 75), and it seems Conan Doyle may have included this to bring a shiver of excitement and fear to his readers.

TOP TIP: CONAN DOYLE'S USE OF IRONY (A02)

Though the case seems to have taken another serious turn, Conan Doyle injects humour into the novella on many occasions. We are entertained, alongside Holmes and Watson, by the newspaper account of the events of the night before. Reread the section from page 71, 'About twelve o' clock last night', to page 72, 'What do you think of it?' Consider how Athelney Jones has been portrayed in the news article; the irony in the reporting of his methods, compared to his actual methods in Chapter 5; and the irony of him being presented as having 'a single vigorous and masterful mind' (p. 72). Make some notes and then explain why Holmes concludes, 'Isn't it gorgeous!' (p. 72), after reading the report.

KEY CONTEXT (A03)

In the book that Holmes refers to, there is no mention of why the Andaman peoples might have wished to defend themselves against the 'British official'. Nor is there any criticism of those who sought to 'win them over' and colonise their islands (p. 75). The account is negative in its portrayal of the islanders. It gives us very clear indications of the prejudiced attitudes at the time.

KEY QUOTATION: DIALOGUE AND CLASS (A03)

Mrs Smith is just one of the working-class characters in the novella. Conan Doyle reveals this to us through her use of dialect words, which contrast with the precise standard English of Holmes. He comments to Watson, 'The main thing with people of that sort … is never to let them think that their information can be of the slightest importance to you' (p. 69). Holmes has relied on 'people of that sort' through the novella to help him. The suggestion here is that they are mere accessories.

CHAPTER 9: A BREAK IN THE CHAIN

SUMMARY

- Watson visits Mrs Forrester and Miss Morstan to update them on the case.
- Holmes spends the night pacing his room, anxious about the lack of progress in the search for the steam launch.
- A day passes with no news and Holmes takes up the search for the suspects himself.
- Athelney Jones arrives at Baker Street after receiving a telegram from Holmes.
- An old sailor, claiming to have news, visits Watson and Jones.
- The sailor turns out to be Holmes in disguise.
- Holmes issues orders to Jones, before inviting him to stay for dinner.

TOP TIP **A01**

Keep track of the different ways that Watson presents Holmes's character. Note his different views of Holmes – sometimes he sees him as a genius, at others as irritating, egotistical or opinionated. Consider how Holmes has been presented as a well-rounded, convincing character as a result. Make notes on what this also reveals about Watson himself.

WHY IS THIS CHAPTER IMPORTANT?

A The **halt** in developments provides **tension** following the **fast-paced events** we have witnessed so far.

B Watson and the reader are able to **speculate** as to whether Holmes will actually be able to solve this case.

C Athelney Jones is brought back into the plot to act in a **supporting role** to Holmes.

KEY STRUCTURE: DESPAIR AND DELAY **A02**

We learn that Watson has slept until 'late in the afternoon' (p. 77). Holmes, however, has apparently not slept for the second night in a row. Conan Doyle uses the passing of time in this chapter as an indicator of Holmes's fixation on the case and inability to rest until more progress is made. A third night passes where Holmes is reduced to looking 'worn and haggard', 'feverish' (p. 79). A fourth passes where he engages in scientific experiment until 'the small hours' (p. 80) and yet is up at dawn ready to restart the search himself in 'sailor dress' (p. 81).

Conan Doyle uses the **device** of texts within the text to move the plot forward. Watson reads the newspaper and finds news of Thaddeus Sholto's release. He then sees a missing person's 'advertisement in the agony column' for Mordecai Smith (p. 82) – with a full description of the launch. Both of these texts are shared with the reader. Later we are allowed to read the telegram that Holmes has sent to Athelney Jones summoning him to Baker Street. A further device of disguise is used to suggest the case may soon be solved: 'I knows all about it' states the old sailor (p. 85). The fact that Holmes is in disguise as the sailor adds humour. However, Conan Doyle then puts Holmes back at the centre of organising the action: 'you must put yourself under my orders' he instructs Jones (p. 86) after revealing his true identity.

AIMING HIGH: COMMENTING ON CHANGES IN CHARACTER

In this chapter Holmes slips back into the frustrated mood we saw at the beginning of the **novella**, when he was almost paralysed with boredom. We see how Holmes can plunge into a dark depression when not faced with intellectual challenge and stimulation. His housekeeper worries for his health, as does Watson. Holmes has been described in animalistic terms before with his 'hawk-like features' (p. 12). Here he is rather like a caged animal, pacing his lair, waiting for news that will release him once again into thought and action.

CHECKPOINT 8

At what time and place does Holmes ask for the police boat to be waiting?

Athelney Jones has also undergone a changed perspective. He has lost his suspect in Thaddeus Sholto. His pompous and bombastic nature has been subdued by his failure to close the case. He is described as 'downcast', 'meek' and 'even apologetic' (p. 83). Jones becomes tamed in this chapter. Once Holmes reverts back to a position of power and authority, Jones submits to his command 'Entirely' (p. 87).

CHAPTER 10: THE END OF THE ISLANDER

SUMMARY

- Holmes, Watson and Jones enjoy a pleasant supper together before setting out to capture their suspects.
- They board the police boat and travel to Jacobson's yard where Holmes has located the *Aurora*.
- On the way, Holmes explains how he discovered its whereabouts.
- The *Aurora* leaves the yard and steams swiftly down the Thames, pursued by the police boat.
- As they gain on the *Aurora*, it is clear that Jonathan Small is on board with his accomplice who is a small black man.
- As Small's accomplice makes to shoot a poison dart, Watson and Holmes fire their pistols and he is killed.
- Small forces the boat towards the shore, where he attempts to escape on foot, but is captured.

TOP TIP (A02)

Look back at page 89 where Watson describes the supper. Note the changes in both Holmes's and Jones's characters here and the vocabulary used to describe them. How is this a contrast to how they have previously been presented?

WHY IS THIS CHAPTER IMPORTANT?

A The **hunt** for **Mordecai Smith** and the **steam launch** is over.

B Jonathan Small is **captured** and the **treasure recovered**.

KEY THEME: THE SAVAGE VERSUS THE CIVILISED (A01)

Throughout the novella, we have seen fear and prejudice about places and peoples thought of as foreign. Britain, at the time, had power over many colonies: the native populations of those places were often seen as a threat to that power. In this chapter we see how Small's loyal accomplice (who has not even been named by this point in the novella) is described as a 'savage, distorted creature' (p. 96). Much of the vocabulary used to describe Tonga is connected with animalistic imagery such as 'bestiality and cruelty' and 'half animal fury' (p. 97).

By presenting Tonga in this way, Conan Doyle seems to justify the swift and brutal way he is shot by Holmes and Watson. He is seen as less than human, and therefore his life is not valued. Watson describes him as a creature to be feared, not as a stranger to this land, who is likely to be fearful himself. In this way, we learn a great deal about how people of colour were perceived at the time. We can also see how racial prejudice was common even among the most educated members of society such as the doctor and Holmes.

KEY CONTEXT (A03)

Think about how Conan Doyle presents the working classes in this chapter, by making notes about what is suggested by these quotations: 'That is usually a product of higher education' (p. 91); 'He was rather the worse for liquor' (p. 92); 'Dirty-looking rascals' (p. 94).

EXAM FOCUS: COMMENTING ON THE USE OF LANGUAGE TO CREATE TENSION

As the chase continues along the river, Conan Doyle increases the pace of the story again and raises the tension. Here is an example of a student pinpointing how this happens through Conan Doyle's language choices:

> Holmes is presented as being in command and uses imperatives 'Heap it on, stokers!' (p. 94), 'Pile it on, men, pile it on!' (p. 95) to suggest his desperation to increase speed. Industrial images are used and onomatopoeic verbs to describe how the 'furnaces roared' and 'whizzed' and 'clanked' (p. 94). We are given the impression that Holmes is pushing the men and boat to their limits to catch their suspects. In contrast, the boat is described as having 'sprang and quivered like a living thing' (p. 95) and we are reminded of a hunt by Watson referring to the suspects as 'our quarry' (p. 97). He compares the chase to other hunts he has taken part in, 'never did sport give me such a wild thrill as this ... man-hunt' (p. 96).

Has a firm focus on what the writer is doing and shows subject knowledge through confident, accurate use of terminology

Considers the impact on the reader

Ranges through the chapter to find short, apt, judicious quotations

Now you try it:

Write a paragraph exploring the way tension is created in a different episode of the novella. Chapter 3 or Chapter 5 would be useful sources for this task. Start: *Conan Doyle creates tension in …*

CHAPTER 11: THE GREAT AGRA TREASURE

CHECKPOINT 9

Where was Jonathan Small trying to get to aboard Mordecai Smith's boat that evening?

SUMMARY

- Small has been captured and is on board the police boat.
- He is encouraged to tell his story honestly by Holmes.
- Watson is entrusted with the box of treasure to deliver to Miss Morstan.
- Watson finds Miss Morstan alone and presents her with the box.
- On forcing the lock, the box is found to be empty.
- Watson declares his love for Miss Morstan.

WHY IS THIS CHAPTER IMPORTANT?

A We meet **Jonathan Small**, who is **calm** and **resigned**.

B We see how Small is treated in **contrast** to how Tonga was treated.

C The loss of the treasure means it cannot cause any further **misery**.

D The **relationship** between Watson and Miss Morstan is established.

TOP TIP: WRITING ABOUT MISS MORSTAN

Mary Morstan has a central role in the novella as the person who brings the case to light, provides all of the background details and comforts the housekeeper. Despite her initial confidence, she is later presented as being stereotypically weak and fragile herself: 'she turned so white that I feared that she was about to faint' (p. 103) as Watson tells her of the chase on the Thames. Miss Morstan is always presented through the eyes of the men in the novella: Watson, Holmes and ultimately through the writer himself.

KEY CONTEXT: THE ANGEL IN THE HOUSE (A03)

'The Angel in the House' is a term used to describe the perfect Victorian middle-class woman. It is taken from a poem written at the time, which presents a man's view of his perfect wife. In this era, women were expected to focus on the home and domestic life. They were often presented as being completely helpless where matters of business or action were concerned. In *The Sign of the Four*, we can see how all of the women are connected with their homes and are rarely involved in the action of the plot. Even when Miss Morstan ventures across London on the first night of the investigation, she is placed in Watson's care (Ch. 3). At Pondicherry Lodge she is left to comfort the housekeeper while the action takes place (Ch. 5).

The home was also seen as the place where women would be protected from the dangers of the outside world and where men could return to enjoy the comfort they provided. Look at the description of Miss Morstan on page 102. She is dressed in a 'white diaphanous material' like an angel and has a 'sweet, grave face' according to Watson's perspective. His arrival causes her to have 'a bright flush of surprise and of pleasure'. At the end of the chapter, she is referred to as his 'treasure' (p. 105), a valuable prize that he has rightfully gained.

REVISION FOCUS: TRACKING THE AGRA TREASURE

The treasure has been seen as the rightful property of Miss Morstan from the beginning of the case. Small, however, thinks he has 'a fair claim ... upon half a million' (p. 101). Work back through the novella, tracing who has held the treasure at various points in the story. Present your findings on a flow chart. Add notes about their reasons for having the treasure and whether their motives were good or dishonest. Now, read on to Chapter 12 to continue tracing the history of the treasure.

TOP TIP (A01)

Jones says, 'If we are pretty quick in catching our men, we are not so quick in condemning them' (p. 101). Holmes offers Small a cigar and a drink from his hip flask, 'for you are very wet' (p. 100). Consider how both Holmes and Jones have treated other characters in the novella on capture. Is Jones's statement correct?

CHAPTER 12: THE STRANGE STORY OF JONATHAN SMALL

SUMMARY

- Watson returns to Baker Street to find Holmes, Jones and Small.
- Small confesses to having scattered the treasure in the River Thames.
- He tells the story of his past, from joining the army and being posted to India.
- Small tells of how he lost his leg in an attack by a crocodile.
- He describes his job as an overseer on a plantation and how his experience of the Indian Mutiny led him back into military service.
- It was whilst on guard duty that he became involved in the plot to steal the treasure and murder the servant who was transporting it.
- Convicted for murder and imprisoned on the Andaman Islands, he sought help from two British officers.
- Captain Morstan and Major Sholto agreed to help recover the treasure for a share.
- Major Sholto betrayed his accomplices and returned to England with the treasure.
- Small escaped with the help of an Andaman native he had befriended – Tonga.
- He tracked down Major Sholto, leading to the events Holmes has been investigating for Miss Morstan.
- Jones takes Small into custody, leaving Watson to tell Holmes of his marriage proposal to Miss Morstan, and Holmes to reach for his cocaine bottle.

KEY CONTEXT **A03**

Why was a British soldier such as Small sent to India in the first place? Do some Sherlock Holmes detective work of your own. Find out why Britain needed soldiers to be posted to India. What were they protecting? Why were Indian troops also in the British army? What can you discover about the East India Company?

WHY IS THIS CHAPTER IMPORTANT?

A We hear **Small's story** of his experiences in **India**.

B We learn that the treasure was **stolen property** from an **Indian rajah**.

C We find out the **significance** of the **Sign of the Four**.

KEY STRUCTURE: ANOTHER STORY **A0.**

Though the rest of the novella operates chronologically and is narrated by Watson, like many chapters, this one rests on another character telling their story. Just as Miss Morstan has a story to tell in Chapter 2 and Thaddeus Sholto a story to tell in Chapter 4, Small's story is the one that brings resolution to the case. Small's story takes in his whole life from being a young man, joining the army to escape 'a mess over a girl' (p. 109) and being posted abroad to India. It takes the reader on a further journey – this time not through London – but to a distant and foreign land.

Small presents true historical events in his **narrative**, notably the Indian Mutiny of 1857. Small's narrative acts almost as a complete short story in itself and has many elements of a wild adventure within it: a young man leaving home, a foreign country, an escape from a crocodile, treasure, a spell in prison, escape and revenge. As we move back into the main plot, it seems as though Small's 'Strange Story' acts almost like a **fable** or morality tale, a warning to readers of the dangers of such an adventurous life.

AIMING HIGH: COMMENTING ON BRITISH VALUES ⭐

In the novella there are many examples of Indian characters being treated differently to the native British characters. Nowhere is this more evident than with the brutal shooting of Tonga compared to Small's arrest. Small is given a cigar and a warming drink from Holmes's hip flask. There are other smaller, but no less important instances too. At the end of the novella, an assumption is made that Sholto's Indian butler can have been the only one responsible for aiding Small (p. 133). The British are seen as acting honourably – even on the occasions when they clearly are not. Small is portrayed as honourable for wishing to uphold the safety of the Agra fort, even when he is about to aid in the murder of Achmet (p. 114). In reality, the Mutiny meant atrocities were committed on both sides, yet British troops are presented as heroic. They held their ground despite being outnumbered, 'the millions against the hundreds' (p. 111).

Major Sholto, a British officer, is the one who takes the treasure from India, its rightful home. The treasure could be seen as a **metaphor** for why the British were in India in the first place – to gain wealth. Remember that initially the treasure belonged to an Indian rajah, who was 'driven out of India' (p. 122) after the uprising.

KEY QUOTATION: SEEKING A FORTUNE (A01)

Abdullah Khan gives Jonathan Small little choice but to join their plot to steal the jewels. However, he makes a serious comment when he suggests, 'We only ask you to do that which your countrymen come to this land for. We ask you to be rich' (p. 114). Khan recognises that the British have colonised India for one reason only – to make themselves wealthy through exploiting the natural resources of the land.

KEY CONTEXT: THE INDIAN MUTINY (A03)

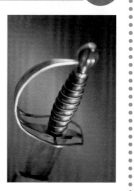

This term refers to a rebellion in India in 1857 against the East India Company, which controlled much of India at the time. It began as an uprising by Indian troops (sepoys) against their officers and escalated into a number of violent and brutal clashes. It led to the East India Company being disbanded and the British government taking complete control of India. This was called the British Raj and led to Queen Victoria being named Empress of India.

CHECKPOINT 10 (A01)

What were the names of the three accomplices whom Small joined in order to steal the Agra treasure?

TOP TIP (A01)

At the end of the novella Jones concludes, 'duty is duty, and I have gone rather far in doing what you and your friend asked me' (p. 131). Make a list of the unusual requests Jones grants Holmes to enable the investigation to end successfully.

PROGRESS AND REVISION CHECK

SECTION ONE: CHECK YOUR KNOWLEDGE

Answer these quick questions to test your basic knowledge of the novella, its characters and events:

1. What object does Watson give to Holmes to test out his theories?

2. What is the name of Holmes's housekeeper?

3. Where was Captain Morstan staying when he telegraphed his daughter?

4. On what date was the anonymous letter posted to Miss Morstan?

5. Who meets Miss Morstan, Holmes and Watson at the theatre?

6. What drink does Thaddeus Sholto offer Miss Morstan?

7. Why does Major Sholto keep Captain Morstan's death a secret?

8. What time do the main characters reach Pondicherry Lodge?

9. Who has a room that is 'fitted out as a chemical laboratory'?

10. Why does Holmes ask Watson to sit in the corner when they gain access to the locked room?

11. What has been used to kill Bartholomew Sholto?

12. Where does Holmes send Watson once he has escorted Miss Morstan home?

13. What type of dog is Toby?

14. Why did Jonathan Small not collect the treasure himself, according to Holmes in Chapter 7?

15. Whose boatyard do Holmes and Watson stop to make enquiries at?

16. What is the name of the boy who leads the Baker Street Irregulars?

17. What does Holmes do while he waits for news of the *Aurora*?

18. How many boatyards did Holmes check before finding the *Aurora*?

19. Why does Watson say 'Thank God!' when he realises the treasure box is empty?

20. Why was Major Sholto so eager to take the Agra treasure for himself?

PROGRESS AND REVISION CHECK

SECTION TWO: CHECK YOUR UNDERSTANDING

Here are two tasks about the significance of particular moments in the novella. These require more thought and slightly longer responses. In each case, try to write at least three to four paragraphs.

Task 1: In Chapter One we are introduced to Holmes and to our narrator, Watson. Think about:

- What the chapter reveals about the character of Holmes
- How Conan Doyle presents the relationship between Holmes and Watson

Task 2: In Chapter Five, the setting of Pondicherry Lodge is very mysterious. Think about:

- What the setting of Pondicherry Lodge adds to the tension of the story
- How Conan Doyle presents Pondicherry Lodge to add to the excitement for the reader

PROGRESS CHECK

GOOD PROGRESS

I can:

- understand how Conan Doyle has sequenced and revealed events. ☐
- refer to the importance of key events in the novella. ☐
- select well-chosen evidence, including key quotations, to support my ideas. ☐

EXCELLENT PROGRESS

I can:

- refer in depth to the main and minor events and how they contribute to the development of the plot. ☐
- understand how Conan Doyle has carefully ordered or revealed events for particular effects. ☐
- draw on a range of carefully selected key evidence, including quotations, to support my ideas. ☐

WHO'S WHO?

Mrs Forrester

Miss Morstan

Mrs Hudson

Dr Watson

Sherlock Holmes

Athelney Jones

Thaddeus Sholto

Toby, Mr Sherman's dog

Jonathan Small

Mr Sherman

Tonga

The Baker Street Irregulars

SHERLOCK HOLMES

SHERLOCK HOLMES'S ROLE IN THE NOVELLA

Sherlock Holmes is a highly intelligent detective, based in London in the late nineteenth century. Despite his genius, he has flaws in his character. He can be arrogant and lack social skills. During the novella he:

- is seen to inject cocaine when he is bored and restless (Ch. 1).
- becomes immediately engaged in activity when Miss Morstan presents her case (Ch. 2).
- investigates the crime scene at Pondicherry Lodge in a detailed, forensic way (Chs 5–6).
- constructs a plan to catch the suspects (Ch. 9).
- takes charge of the regular police force, through Athelney Jones, to capture the suspects (Chs 9–10).

EXAM FOCUS: WRITING ABOUT SHERLOCK HOLMES

Key point	Evidence/Further meaning
Holmes is considered to be something of a genius in his field and thrives on having difficult cases to solve.	<ul><li>'My mind … rebels at stagnation. Give me problems, give me work' (p. 2)</li><li>Suggests that Holmes is easily bored and is only content when he has something to work on.</li></ul>
He can be somewhat arrogant in his views and dismissive of the views and ideas of others.	<ul><li>'On the contrary … I only require a few missing links to have an entirely connected case' (p. 41)</li><li>Holmes is always one step ahead of Watson, the police inspector and the reader.</li></ul>
Holmes focuses on the rational and the logical and has little time for emotions or feelings.	<ul><li>'"You really are an automaton,– a calculating machine!" I cried. "There is something positively inhuman about you at times"' (p. 15)</li><li>Holmes can hurt Watson's feelings through his lack of sensitivity, for example in regard to his brother and his marriage to Miss Morstan.</li></ul>

TOP TIP: WRITING ABOUT SHERLOCK HOLMES (A01)

When writing about Holmes think about how he is the motivating force in both the novella and the investigation. His capacity for deep thought, analysis and stamina contrasts with characters such as Watson and Jones. Note how the action slows down at the point he is relying on news from others. Only when he takes matters into his own hands and locates the *Aurora* does the plot increase in pace and excitement once again.

DR WATSON

DR WATSON'S ROLE IN THE NOVELLA

Watson is the narrator of the story. Everything is seen through his eyes. He is Holmes's patient friend, with whom he shares lodgings at 221b Baker Street. A doctor by profession, Watson has a background in the army as a surgeon. During the novella he:

- has concerns about Holmes's health and well-being (Chs 1/9).
- questions Holmes's methods and approaches (Ch. 1).
- acts as Holmes's assistant in solving the case and catching the suspects (Chs 3–7/10).
- shows his romantic nature through his growing love for Miss Morstan (Chs 2/7/11).

EXAM FOCUS: WRITING ABOUT DR WATSON

Key point	Evidence/Further meaning
Watson knows Holmes, his cases and his methods well and has used them as a basis for story writing.	<ul><li>'I even embodied it in a small brochure with the somewhat fantastic title of "A Study in Scarlet"' (p. 3)</li><li>Watson takes on the role of narrator and even fictional author, *A Study in Scarlet* also being a novel by Conan Doyle featuring Holmes and Watson.</li></ul>
Watson is more sensitive than Holmes and acknowledges and shows his feelings much more easily.	<ul><li>'I sprang from my chair and limped impatiently about the room with considerable bitterness in my heart' (p. 8)</li><li>Holmes at times can be hurtful to Watson. He criticises Watson's writing, is insensitive about his brother's death and is dismissive when Watson announces his engagement to Miss Morstan.</li></ul>
Though without Holmes's powers of deduction, Watson is a loyal assistant to Holmes and is keen to take part in the action, even when dangerous.	<ul><li>'"I should like, however, to see the matter through with you, now that I have got so far." "Your presence will be of great service to me," he answered' (p. 51)</li><li>Watson is very much part of the action at Pondicherry Lodge and in the final chase along the Thames where he fires his revolver at Tonga.</li></ul>

TOP TIP: WRITING ABOUT DR WATSON

Watson can be seen as a contrast to Holmes. He is more conservative and more consistent than Holmes, who switches rapidly between dark depression and frenetic action. Like Holmes, however, Watson is observant. Though he praises Holmes's 'extraordinary genius for minutiae' (p. 5) he too recounts the events of the case in detail. Watson, however, is more humble, 'What was I, an army surgeon with a weak leg and a weaker banking-account, that I should dare to think of such things?' (p. 16).

MISS MORSTAN

MISS MORSTAN'S ROLE IN THE NOVELLA

Mary Morstan is the central female character in the novella and it is through her that the mystery is established. The daughter of Captain Morstan, she is presented as being of good character and extremely sensible. She is also the romantic interest, captivating Watson from his first meeting with her. In the novella she:

- seeks Holmes's help after receiving an anonymous letter (Ch. 2).
- presents a mystery having received a number of pearls on the same date each year for the past six years (Ch. 2).
- has a father who disappeared ten years earlier (Ch. 2).
- travels with Holmes and Watson to meet Thaddeus Sholto.
- is relieved and pleased when the treasure box is empty.
- returns Watson's love.

EXAM FOCUS: WRITING ABOUT MISS MORSTAN

Key point	Evidence/Further meaning
Miss Morstan earns Holmes's respect by being methodical and organised, having kept hold of all the letters as evidence.	• 'You are certainly a model client. You have the correct intuition' (p. 14) • Holmes praises the qualities in Miss Morstan that he finds useful, in contrast to the way that Watson views her – as a romantic proposition.
Mary is praised for her sensitive nature and calm, composed manner, which were seen at the time as attractive qualities in Victorian women.	• 'She must have been more than woman if she did not feel some uneasiness … yet her self-control was perfect' (p. 18) • Watson finds it almost surprising that a woman can cope with the night's adventures through London.
Mary rejects the corrupting influence of the treasure. She is calm on discovering the box is empty.	• '"The treasure is lost," said Miss Morstan, calmly.' (p. 104) • Mary is shown to be more civilised than the greedy men for whom it has only brought misery.

AIMING HIGH: MORALITY IN THE NOVELLA

Mary acts as a moral yardstick in the novella by which we can measure the behaviour and motivation of others. The fact she has no desire for the treasure and does not anticipate its arrival with greed sets her apart from the four thieves and from her own father and Major Sholto. Mary, however, has not been subject to what many readers at the time would have seen as the 'uncivilising' influence of British India.

THADDEUS SHOLTO

THADDEUS SHOLTO'S ROLE IN THE NOVELLA

Thaddeus Sholto is the son of Major Sholto and twin brother of Bartholomew. He is portrayed as an unusual character due to his appearance and lifestyle. Though we are sympathetic to him, he brings a comic element to the novella. In the novella he:

- believes Miss Morstan should have her rightful share of the treasure as Captain Morstan's heir.
- has sent the pearl each year to Miss Morstan.
- is responsible for the anonymous letter.
- is a contrast to his brother Bartholomew, who, like Major Sholto, is keen to keep the treasure for himself.

EXAM FOCUS: WRITING ABOUT THADDEUS SHOLTO

Key point	Evidence/Further meaning
The rich furnishings of Thaddeus's house create a strange and surprising image of the man and his lifestyle.	• 'Pray step into my little sanctum … An oasis of art in the howling desert of South London' (p. 23) • Thaddeus is aligning himself with the Aesthetic Movement of the time.
Thaddeus appears to be fair and good-hearted. He has wanted Miss Morstan to have her share of the treasure since he learned of its existence.	• 'Besides, it would have been such bad taste to have treated a young lady in so scurvy a fashion' (p. 31) • Thaddeus sees that keeping the treasure from Miss Morstan is not in line with the cultured way he likes to live.
Athelney Jones almost immediately accuses Thaddeus of his brother's murder.	• 'You see that I am weaving my web round Thaddeus' (p. 49) • This allows Holmes to challenge Jones's assumptions and assure Thaddeus he will work to free him.

AIMING HIGH: EXPLORE THE AESTHETIC MOVEMENT

Through Thaddeus, Conan Doyle seems to be gently teasing the Aesthetic Movement. This was an artistic movement of the late nineteenth century that celebrated 'art for art's sake'. Thaddeus is very proud of his art collection, 'I may call myself a patron of the arts' (p. 26), but he also represents the values of the movement in his furnishings and rich fabrics. His taste for the 'aesthetic' extends to his elaborate form of dress, with his 'very long befrogged topcoat with Astrakhan collar and cuffs' (p. 32), and his habit of smoking from a hookah (a pipe used in the East).

JONATHAN SMALL

JONATHAN SMALL'S ROLE IN THE NOVELLA

Jonathan Small is one of 'The Four'. He is a former soldier posted to India. Small was imprisoned on the Andaman Islands as a result of his part in the murder of Achmet the merchant. Whilst in prison, he planned to regain the treasure for the four, by asking for help from the British officers. His betrayal by Major Sholto led to the events in the novella. During the novella he:

- has tracked down Major Sholto and frightened him to death.
- breaks into Pondicherry Lodge, with Tonga, and retrieves the treasure.
- hires the *Aurora* from Mordecai Smith's boatyard to aid his escape.
- is chased by Holmes, Watson and Jones in the police boat.
- is captured and confesses his crimes.
- disposes of the treasure in the Thames before anyone else can take it.

EXAM FOCUS: WRITING ABOUT JONATHAN SMALL (A01)

Key point	Evidence/Further meaning
Small tries to safeguard the interests of the three men he made the pact with.	● 'It's been the sign of four with us always' (p. 107) ● This shows Small's sense of honour is stronger than Major Sholto's who was dismissive of Small's accomplices because of their race.
Small also tries to demonstrate to Holmes, Watson and Jones that he did not put the British occupants of the fort in any danger, nor was he prepared to do so.	● 'if it's anything against the safety of the fort I will have no truck with it' (p. 114) ● Despite his concern for the inhabitants of the fort, he showed no mercy to Achmet as he delivered the treasure to the fort, or to the convict guard he killed to secure his escape.
Once he realises he will be captured Small scatters the treasure in the Thames to prevent anyone else from having it.	● 'I cannot bear to feel that I have paid this price only that another may enjoy it!' (p. 108) ● Small comments on the injustice that the treasure is not his after the hardships he suffered in the Andaman Islands.

KEY QUOTATION: BETRAYAL AND REVENGE (A01)

Small insists that the treasure is rightfully his: 'It is my treasure; and if I can't have the loot I'll take darned good care that no one else does' (p. 107), justifying why he throws it into the Thames. It is the betrayal by Major Sholto that he finds hardest to bear. He entrusted Sholto with the location of the treasure, who then betrayed both Morstan and 'the four'. Small sees the treasure as 'a curse' (p. 101) but does not recognise that it was stolen from an Indian rajah. Even from his lowly position, he feels he has a right to a share of India's wealth.

ATHELNEY JONES

ATHELNEY JONES'S ROLE IN THE NOVELLA

Jones is a detective from Scotland Yard. There is some good-natured rivalry between the two detectives however. Jones is somewhat scornful of Holmes's methods but is ready to praise his genius towards the end of the novella. During the novella he:

- visits the crime scene at Pondicherry Lodge and engages in a humorous exchange with Holmes.
- arrests members of the Sholto household in connection with Bartholomew's death.
- features in an exaggerated newspaper report of his successful investigation.
- is forced to admit to Watson his inquiry has no leads.
- is persuaded to join forces with Holmes and supply him with a police launch.
- takes part in the chase along the Thames and arrests Jonathan Small.

EXAM FOCUS: WRITING ABOUT ATHELNEY JONES

Key point	Evidence/Further meaning
As a representative of Scotland Yard and the police force, Jones is made to seem clumsy in comparison to Holmes's careful work and thoughtful approach.	<ul><li>'Heavy steps and the clamor of loud voices were audible from below, and the hall door shut with a loud crash' (p. 47)</li><li>This contrasts with the way Holmes has prevented even Watson from stepping into the crime scene and disturbing evidence.</li></ul>
Jones is suspicious of Holmes's methods and feels his work is based on theory and not police practice.	<ul><li>'Stern facts here,– no room for theories' (p. 48)</li><li>This is ironic as Jones jumps to conclusions and makes random arrests with no hard evidence.</li></ul>
As Jones's own investigation leads nowhere, he is forced to admit to needing Holmes's help.	<ul><li>'It's a very dark case, and my professional credit is at stake. I should be very glad of a little assistance' (p. 83)</li><li>This describes a less pompous side to Jones and shows how the two detectives work together.</li></ul>
Once Small is safely in custody, Jones shows signs of his initial tendency to act in a superior manner.	<ul><li>'It was amusing to notice how the consequential Jones was already beginning to give himself airs on the strength of the capture' (p. 101)</li><li>Holmes and Watson don't take this aspect of his behaviour seriously and the men remain friendly towards each other.</li></ul>

MINOR CHARACTERS

TONGA

Tonga, a native of the Andaman Islands, is referred to on numerous occasions in the novella – for example in connection with Bartholomew's murder and as Small's accomplice. However, throughout the whole novella we do not hear from him at all. He is brutally shot without being able to give an account of himself. The terms used to disparage him reveal racial prejudice. Tonga is an important character because he represents how even the most educated of people at the end of the nineteenth century (such as Watson and Holmes) viewed some of the people in the colonies. This is a view we would find disturbing today.

MAJOR SHOLTO

Despite being an officer serving in the army and representing Britain overseas, Major Sholto appears as a dishonourable character. We learn that he squandered his money in playing cards and gambling. He then saw a way out of his situation by betraying the trust of both Small and his close friend Morstan. He keeps the treasure for himself, though clearly it has brought him no joy. He seems to have lived in fear for the rest of his life and only tried to make amends on his death-bed.

BARTHOLOMEW SHOLTO

Son of Major Sholto and twin brother of Thaddeus, we only 'meet' Bartholomew as the murder victim at Pondicherry Lodge. We learn that he is a contrast to his brother Thaddeus and shared some of his father's greedy characteristics. He was single minded in trying to locate the treasure and did not want to share it with Miss Morstan.

CAPTAIN MORSTAN

Again, a character we only meet through reputation, Captain Morstan's mysterious disappearance signifies the start of the mystery. He disappeared ten years before his daughter, Miss Morstan, consults with Holmes. We learn about his relationship with Major Sholto and the true facts of his death from Thaddeus Sholto. He too has a somewhat questionable reputation in that he also agreed to take part in the plot to recover the treasure.

'THE FOUR'

Jonathan Small made a pact with three Indian co-conspirators to steal the Agra treasure. His three accomplices are Abdullah Khan, Mahomet Singh and Dost Akbar. They justify taking the rajah's treasure so it does not fall into the hands of the East India Company. They are portrayed in the novella as fearless, strong and somewhat brutal but also with a strict sense of honour to each other. All of the four are imprisoned for their actions.

TOP TIP (A01)

Look back at all of the characters who have a connection with the Agra treasure: 'The Four', Tonga, the Sholto family, the Morstans. Make some notes on how the treasure has had an impact on all of their lives.

TOP TIP (A01)

Think about the different characteristics Conan Doyle gives to the different classes of people in the novella and how far they are stereotypical. Make notes on how the working-class characters are described compared to the middle-class characters. Where do the British officers fit in this comparison? Do they match the stereotypes?

MRS CECIL FORRESTER

Mrs Forrester employs Miss Morstan as a governess. However, the two women seem to be close friends. It is Mrs Forrester who has recommended Holmes to Miss Morstan. Like Miss Morstan, she is presented as a symbol of perfect feminine qualities. Her home is seen as a sanctuary from the 'wild dark business' (p. 54) of the case.

MRS HUDSON

Mrs Hudson is the landlady and housekeeper at 221b Baker Street. She is taken aback by the arrival of the Baker Street Irregulars on her doorstep. However, she is clearly concerned for the well-being of her lodgers and she shares her worries with Watson about Holmes staying awake all night.

THE SMITHS

Mordecai Smith's boatyard is a central clue to the development of the plot and his disappearance along with his steam launch help to change the pace of the story. He is a working-class character who is presented as drinking too much when he has money. His wife and son are easily convinced to share information with the gentleman detective Holmes.

THE STAFF OF PONDICHERRY LODGE

We meet another colourful working-class character at Pondicherry Lodge – McMurdo the prizefighter. His presence shows how concerned Major Sholto was about his security and McMurdo tells us he was well paid to keep the property safe. There is an unusual, almost comic twist when it is discovered Holmes knows McMurdo, having fought him in a charity match. This gains everyone immediate access to Pondicherry Lodge. Mrs Bernstone is the housekeeper, another female character who is not part of the action, but presented as fearful and in need of care from Miss Morstan to whom she turns with gratitude. We do not meet Lal Rao the butler, who is later discovered to have helped Small. Major Sholto's loyal servant Lal Chowdar, who helped to dispose of Captain Morstan's body, is dead.

MR SHERMAN AND TOBY

Mr Sherman is another one of Sherlock Holmes's working-class acquaintances for whom the mention of Holmes's name means they will answer requests for help. He is the owner of the strange shop in Pinchin Lane which Watson visits to borrow Toby, the keen tracker dog used to help trace the suspects through London.

THE BAKER STREET IRREGULARS

Led by Wiggins, this is a group of poor London boys. Holmes employs them them to be his 'eyes' and 'ears' on the streets of London. He has a lot of confidence in their ability but, in this case, is forced to take on the search for the Aurora himself.

PROGRESS AND REVISION CHECK

SECTION ONE: CHECK YOUR KNOWLEDGE

1 What is the name of the housekeeper at Pondicherry Lodge?

2 Who did Captain Morstan visit on his return from India?

3 Thaddeus Sholto has a twin brother – what is his name?

4 Which member of staff at Pondicherry Lodge greets Holmes?

5 What is the name of the shopkeeper on Pinchin Lane who Watson visits to collect Toby?

6 Who is described as 'not a bad fellow' in Chapter 8?

7 Who is the leader of the Baker Street Irregulars?

8 What are the names of Jonathan Small's three co-conspirators?

9 Who does Small hire a boat from?

10 Who does Small describe as 'stanch [staunch] and true' in Chapter 12?

> **TOP TIP** (A01)
>
> Answer these quick questions to test your basic knowledge of the novella's characters.

SECTION TWO: CHECK YOUR UNDERSTANDING

Task: How does Conan Doyle convey the character of Sherlock Holmes?

Think about:

- His approach to solving the case
- The views of the framework narrator, Watson

> **TOP TIP** (A01)
>
> This task requires more thought and a slightly longer response. Try to write at least three to four paragraphs.

PROGRESS CHECK

GOOD PROGRESS

I can:

- explain the significance of the main characters in how the action develops. ☐
- refer to how they are described by Conan Doyle and how this affects the way we see them. ☐

EXCELLENT PROGRESS

I can:

- analyse in detail how Conan Doyle has shaped and developed characters over the course of the novella. ☐
- infer key ideas, themes and issues from the ways characters and relationships are presented by Conan Doyle. ☐

THEMES

THEME TRACKER (A01)

Crime

- Chapter 4, pp. 27–9: Thaddeus Sholto tells of his father's deathbed confession.
- Chapters 5–6, pp. 40–7: Bartholomew Sholto is murdered and the treasure stolen again.
- Chapter 12, pp. 116–21: 'The Four' murder Achmet and steal the Agra treasure.

CRIME

The theme of crime is central to the focus of the detective story. In *The Sign of the Four* the plot hinges around several crimes:

- By the time we have read to the end of Chapter 12 we discover a number of criminal acts all of which are connected to the Agra treasure. Some of these acts are very brutal indeed, such as the murder of Achmet, 'Ere he could stagger to his feet the Sikh was upon him, and buried his knife twice in his side' (p. 119).
- Others crimes are connected to betrayal, such as that committed by Major Sholto, 'The scoundrel had stolen it all' (p. 127).

Conan Doyle seems to invite the reader to question the motives and morality of the criminals:

- Greed is a motivational factor for some of the crimes that take place in the novella, for example, in Sholto's theft of the treasure.
- At other times revenge is a factor, for example in Small's own brutal murder of the convict guard, 'I struck him full, and knocked the whole front of his skull in' (p. 128).
- In some cases Conan Doyle seems to suggest that circumstances have 'made' criminals out of the characters. In other cases characters are presented as being 'born' criminals. Tonga, for example, is never given the opportunity to speak and confess. Small, somewhat ironically, describes his accomplice as being 'a little blood-thirsty imp' (p. 130), pleased by having unnecessarily killed Bartholomew.

KEY QUOTATION: JUSTICE AND INJUSTICE (AO

Conan Doyle presents us with interesting ideas to think about in terms of justice and injustice in the novella. Jonathan Small is quick to fly at Jones, '"Justice!" snarled the ex-convict. "A pretty justice! Whose loot is this, if it

is not ours?"' (p. 107). He feels he has paid the price for his crime, and should have enjoyed its rewards, with little thought for his two murder victims. Bartholomew Sholto is a murder victim. However, he is presented much less sympathetically because of his greed. Even in death he has a 'ghastly, inscrutable smile' (p. 40). Miss Morstan is also presented as a victim from the beginning, as her father has disappeared. As we discover, her father was part of the continuing plot to steal the treasure. She is never seen as anything but its rightful owner, along with Thaddeus Sholto, yet nothing could be further from the truth.

LOVE AND FRIENDSHIP

The central friendship in the novella is between Holmes and Watson:

- Conan Doyle presents the reader with the consulting detective and his close friend, with whom he shares his ideas and theories. As Watson is our narrator, it means these thoughts are shared with the reader.
- Holmes is rational and logical, Watson more romantic and emotional. In this way, Conan Doyle presents a balanced friendship between the two.

The romantic side of Watson's nature is shown most clearly through his developing love for Miss Morstan:

- They become friends almost immediately.
- Their relationship is presented as being selfless and innocent which makes a contrast to the main plot.

Another significant friendship is that forged between Jonathan Small and his three accomplices: Mahomet Singh, Dost Akbar and Abdullah Khan:

- A code of honour exists between them which Small refuses to break.
- This makes a sharp contrast to the way Sholto betrayed 'The Four', and even his close friend Morstan, to gain the treasure.

THEME TRACKER (A01)

Love and Friendship

- Chapters 1–2, pp. 1–16: Holmes and Watson are shown to have a close friendship.
- Chapter 5, p. 37: Watson falls in love with Miss Morstan.
- Chapter 12, pp. 128–30: Small's friendship with Tonga is not an equal partnership.

EXAM FOCUS: THE VALUE OF FRIENDSHIP   (A01)

In writing about friendship in the novella, it is important to consider who is loyal to their friends and who is not to help show the significance of the theme. Here is an example of a student commenting on this aspect:

> Small and Tonga are shown to have a very strong bond in Chapter 12, even though we are shown that Small seems to have superiority over Tonga, who, 'would do anything to serve me'. This tells us something of the attitudes to race at the time, where a white man would always assume he is superior. Tonga is described as 'stanch and true' by Small, yet he whips him with the rope after Bartholomew's murder. Tonga pays a high price for his loyalty to Small however when he is shot and falls into the river far from home in a foreign land.
>
> This contrasts with the relationship between Morstan and Major Sholto, whose friendship is much less firm and seems to be based on drinking and gambling when they were serving their country. Sholto severs this friendship through his own greed and pays a price for his disloyalty.

Textual references show a confident knowledge of the novella

Contextual ideas are subtly blended in

Perceptive connections and comparisons are made to develop ideas

WEALTH

Wealth seems to be seen as something negative in the novella:

- Miss Morstan is portrayed as a humble governess in the beginning. When Thaddeus Sholto reveals the extent of the wealth potentially due to her, Watson is dismayed, thinking it will put her out of his reach.
- Thaddeus Sholto's home is opulent, filled with exotic treasures and symbols of wealth – probably inherited from his father. In the setting of a London terraced house, however, we are given the impression that this is showy and rather vulgar. There is no indication he is seen as a man of class or taste as a result of his collection.

The desire for wealth is shown to be a corrupting force:

- Both Major and Bartholomew Sholto die painful deaths as a result of their greed. It seems as though there is almost a moral judgement made on them.
- Likewise, none of those connected with the initial theft of the treasure benefits from its wealth, but all languish in prison for many years.

AIMING HIGH: COMMENTING ON THE SIGNIFICANCE OF THE TREASURE

In many respects the treasure is symbolic of India itself. As an important British colony, India was often referred to as the 'jewel in the crown'. In other words India, and the exploitation of its resources, generated huge amounts of wealth for Britain. In *The Sign of the Four* the rajah, who initially owned the treasure, tried to protect the treasure by halving it, and remained neutral in the conflict between the sepoys and the British, believing that whichever side won, he would keep half his wealth. This was not the case however, as he lost everything as a result of the conflict. This is a metaphor for what happened to India itself as it passed completely into British control after the uprising, which was termed a 'Mutiny' by the British.

KEY QUOTATION: GOVERNESS TO HEIRESS (A03)

When Watson revisits Miss Morstan in Chapter 9, Mrs Forrester is delighted at the news, 'Why, Mary, your fortune depends upon the issue of this search. I don't think that you are nearly excited enough. Just imagine what it must be to be rich, and to have the world at your feet!' (p. 78). Many women at the time did not have financial independence. Middle-class married  women did not work and were supported by their husbands. Genteel single women like Miss Morstan could only survive financially by taking employment that was seen to be acceptable. In this case it is the role of governess for a wealthier family. Mrs Forrester appreciates the difference this wealth could make to her friend's life.

DUALITY

In *The Sign of the Four* the pairings of characters can be seen to represent the concept of duality. Duality is when something or someone seems to be made up of two opposing parts.

In this way the male characters of the novella can be viewed in pairs. They represent different characteristics, which could be said to be opposite in nature:

- Holmes represents the scientific and rational mind whilst Watson is the romantic dreamer. Watson is also seen as the one who conforms to moral convention, whilst Holmes has a darker side to his character. Examples of this are his drug use and depression.

- The Sholto twins seem to be presented as a good twin, seeking to make amends for their father's wrongdoing, and an evil twin who retains the father's selfish characteristics.

- Small and Tonga embark on the same mission – to retrieve the treasure – and work as a team. However, Tonga is treated differently as a black man to the way Small is treated as a white man. Small is captured and given the chance to present his side of events. Tonga is brutally shot.

AIMING HIGH: COMMENTING ON OPPOSITIONS

The theme of duality was first developed in some of the early Gothic novels, where good and evil were pitted against each other. Later, the concept of evil became associated with what was primitive or savage, or untamed in man. This helps us to understand some of the fearful attitudes in the novella towards Tonga, for example, 'Never have I seen features so deeply marked with all bestiality and cruelty' (pp. 96–7). We might also contrast how British officers would be perceived at the time – as representing all that is right – against the shameful behaviour of Sholto and Morstan.

The idea developed to explore how one man could be made up of two parts: one part acceptable to society's morals, and another hidden part representing his darkest, perhaps more criminal desires. We see this explored in other texts of the nineteenth century such as *Frankenstein*, *Dr Jekyll and Mr Hyde* and *The Picture of Dorian Gray*. In *The Sign of the Four* this concept can be seen in the swift mood changes Holmes experiences that only his closest friend Watson seems to witness. It is also very clear in the first meeting with

Dr Jekyll and Mr Hyde OF

Thaddeus's murdered twin, 'suspended, as it were, in the air, for all beneath was in shadow, there hung a face,–the very face of our companion Thaddeus' (p. 39).

THEME TRACKER A01

Duality

- Chapters 4–5, pp. 23–45: Thaddeus and his twin Bartholomew are opposing characters.

- Chapter 9, pp. 79–80: Holmes switches from being active to being depressed when there are no further leads in his case.

- Chapter 12, pp. 128–31: Tonga is seen to represent the 'savage' and uncivilised, while Small justifies the murders he commits as being the result of his circumstances.

KEY CONTEXT A03

There was a very strict Victorian code of classifying right and wrong. This caused many people to repress parts of their personality or their desires. If a middle- or upper-class man wished to be respected he had to display very firm morals.

CONTEXTS

KEY CONTEXT (A03)

Charles Darwin's *On the Origin of Species* (1859) caused huge controversy when it was published. His scientific explanations about life on earth contradicted Christian religious beliefs. Contemporary scientific findings led to the development of forensic medicine and analysis. The careful way Holmes investigates a crime scene scientifically and logically reflects this.

THE AUTHOR

Arthur Conan Doyle (see portrait, right) was born in Edinburgh in the middle of the Victorian period in 1859. He went to medical school and trained to be a doctor. Here, Conan Doyle had an influential professor, Dr Joseph Bell, whose methods of diagnosing patients were based on close observation. Bell seems to have partly inspired the character of Holmes. Whilst studying, Conan Doyle began writing stories. His first Sherlock Holmes story, *A Study in Scarlet*, was published in 1887. *The Sign of the Four* was published in 1890. Conan Doyle was a doctor, writer and keen sportsman, and was also interested in politics, spiritualism and social justice.

THE VICTORIAN PERIOD

Queen Victoria ruled Britain from 1837 to 1901 when rapid change took place. Many changes were in medical, scientific and technological fields. Cities expanded with the growth of industries like engineering and textiles. The canal and railway networks were built and coal was mined for steam power. Geographical exploration and expansion also took place and the British Empire grew. British ships traded across the globe. The location of India in *The Sign of the Four* is an example of the opportunities, but also the temptations, the empire provided.

COLONIALISM AND EMPIRE

Britain had been exploring and colonising lands for centuries, but by the nineteenth century the British Empire was vast. It was a global superpower, controlling over a quarter of the Earth's land area and a quarter of its population.

TOP TIP (A01)

Do an internet search for a world map showing the size and extent of the British Empire in the 1880s. Make a note of the countries that Britain had colonised. How do you think this was possible for such a small island? Look closely at the position of India on the map. Note down some ideas as to why you think it was such an important colony for the British.

The British ruling classes had a strong sense of leadership and felt they had a moral responsibility in the world. They believed other countries needed guidance and to be ruled in the way Britain was ruled. The British exported their system of government, the military, the railway system, the English language and their education system. However, many of those who were sent out to rule the colonies did not always have the best interests of the people at heart. The desire to

build wealth for Britain meant that many native peoples and natural resources of the colonised countries were exploited for financial gain. This often stirred up ill feelings and the potential for rebellion such as the Indian Mutiny that Small tells us of in Chapter 12.

ATTITUDES TO RACE

In *The Sign of Four* the presentation of the Indian characters in the novella reflects contemporary views. Though the British had colonised many lands, they were still fearful of rebellion. The native peoples of the lands they occupied far outnumbered the colonisers, as we see when Small reports, 'It was a fight of the millions against the hundreds' (p. 111). In order to justify force, the British needed to view the natives as being somehow inferior and 'savage'. British authorities tried to impose British values, language and religion on native peoples to make them more 'civilised', or so it was thought at the time.

THE CLASS DIVIDE

There was a strong division of the classes during the time the novella is set. We can see this in the contrast between the working-class and middle-class characters. The working classes of the time, particularly in big cities, were employed in industry or in domestic service. The middle and upper classes may not have realised or appreciated the hardships of their working lives. The Victorian middle classes claimed to live by a strict moral code, based on Christian beliefs, hard work, decency, respectability and the value of the family.

WOMEN ON THE MARGINS

There was also a divide in the way women were viewed in Victorian England. Middle-class women were seen to represent all that was good and moral. Marriage was the expected norm for them and they were financially dependent on their fathers and then their husbands. Only if there was no male heir could a woman inherit her father's money. This explains why Mrs Forrester is so pleased for Mary when she learns of the treasure.

KEY CONTEXT (A03)

It is estimated that in the 1850s there were over 8,500 prostitutes working in London. This suggests that many middle- and upper-class men were not adhering to the strict moral code of the time and used prostitutes to explore their repressed sexuality. This unsafe profession for women has links to the darker and more criminal side of London at the time, most famously through the Jack the Ripper case

REVISION FOCUS: EXPLORING CONTEXT

Take each of the following quotations. Make notes on what they tell you about the context of Conan Doyle's novella and how they help us to understand more about the events and the characters themselves:

Holmes and Watson: 'They are coming from work in the yard.' 'Dirty looking rascals, but I suppose every one has some little immortal spark concealed about him.' (p. 94)

Holmes: 'I would not tell them too much,' said Holmes. 'Women are never to be entirely trusted, – not the best of them.' (p. 78)

Small: 'two hundred thousand black devils let loose, and the country was perfect hell.' (p. 110)

SETTINGS

INDIA

India is an important setting in the novella. Everything connected with India initially seems exciting and exotic, including the contents of Thaddeus Sholto's home. India represents mystery. This is most closely symbolised by the missing treasure, known as the Agra treasure. Jonathan Small's story is mainly about India. He shares his experiences with us in Chapter 12, but also reveals some important details about life in colonised India.

LONDON

During the novella we are taken on three exciting journeys through London and each one adds to the mystery and tension of the plot. In each case, the journey takes place at night, which again adds excitement for the reader. Our first journey takes us by coach at speed through London's streets in the evening. Holmes and Watson take a second journey much later that night as they complete their 'six-mile trudge' (p. 58) with Toby. The third journey is again fast and exciting and adds drama as the suspects are chased along the River Thames by boat.

PONDICHERRY LODGE

Pondicherry Lodge is the heavily guarded home of Major Sholto, now occupied by his son Bartholomew. The house has a dark, Gothic feel to it and we have a sense of foreboding as it is described. Not only is the house sinister, but its grounds have been dug over in search of the treasure. It seems an unwelcoming and lonely place. The locked door into Bartholomew's strange laboratory perhaps represents the isolation and fear that the hoarding of the stolen treasure has caused.

221B BAKER STREET

At the famous address shared by Sherlock Holmes and Doctor Watson, Holmes's clients arrive to present their cases, and Holmes experiments and consults his reference books. The Baker Street Irregulars and Athelney Jones are summoned here when their help is required. Mrs Hudson keeps a keen eye on comings and goings as well as looking after Holmes and Watson.

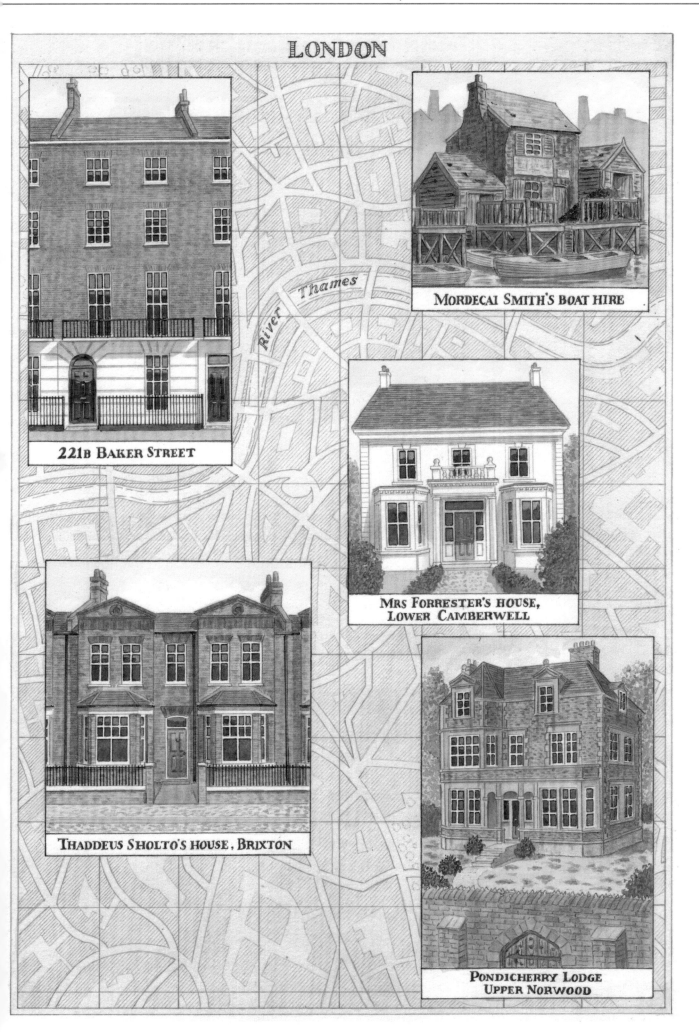

LONDON

221B BAKER STREET

MORDECAI SMITH'S BOAT HIRE

MRS FORRESTER'S HOUSE, LOWER CAMBERWELL

THADDEUS SHOLTO'S HOUSE, BRIXTON

PONDICHERRY LODGE UPPER NORWOOD

PROGRESS AND REVISION CHECK

SECTION ONE: CHECK YOUR KNOWLEDGE

1. What crimes did Jonathan Small have an involvement in?

2. Who has a cynical view of love and marriage?

3. Why is Mrs Forrester pleased that Mary may inherit the treasure?

4. Which characters represent a good twin and an evil twin?

5. Which famous scientist caused controversy with his discoveries in the Victorian era?

6. Which rebellion does Small describe in Chapter 12

7. Which people does Holmes describe sarcastically as 'Nice, amiable people, Watson'?

8. Which famous criminal case highlighted how London had a darker side to it in the Victorian era?

9. Which location is guarded by McMurdo the prizefighter?

10. Which city in India is the treasure named after?

SECTION TWO: CHECK YOUR UNDERSTANDING

How does Conan Doyle present attitudes to wealth in the novella?

Think about:

- What the treasure means to different characters in the novella
- How the author describes the treasure as the novella progresses

PROGRESS CHECK

GOOD PROGRESS

I can:

- explain the main themes, contexts and settings in the text and how they contribute to the effect on the reader. ☐

- use a range of appropriate evidence to support any points I make about these elements. ☐

EXCELLENT PROGRESS

I can:

- analyse in detail the way themes are developed and presented across the novella. ☐
- refer closely to key aspects of context and setting and the implications they have for the author's viewpoint, and the interpretation of relationships and ideas. ☐

FORM

NOVELLA

The Sign of the Four takes the form of a novella. It features some very specific characteristics, which are shared with other works of this genre, published both before and since. A novella is a work of fiction that is shorter than a novel but longer than a short story in that its plot can be more developed, but perhaps has fewer events and twists and complications as a result of its length. It can also introduce a range of interesting characters without examining all of them in close-up. Sometimes novellas are not organised into chapters, though *The Sign of the Four* is. Again, this allows the story to develop in organised, almost bite-sized sections.

THE DETECTIVE STORY

The detective story as a form in Western literature is generally thought to have begun with the writer Edgar Allan Poe in the 1840s. He wrote a number of tales featuring an eccentric detective called August Dupin. Poe's stories are concerned with unravelling the truth of a mystery, through the use of logic and reasoning and close observations. It is clear how Conan Doyle may have adopted this strategy in his own writing and in *The Sign of the Four* through the methods Sherlock Holmes uses.

REVISION FOCUS: THINKING ABOUT THE CONVENTIONS OF THE FORM

Look at some of the established conventions of detective fiction listed below. Make notes on how many of these conventions can be found in *The Sign of the Four*:

1. A crime must be committed – usually theft or murder.

2. The detective should be intellectual, able to piece together the clues to find the motive, the means and the criminal.

3. The detective should have a friend, an accomplice who helps to reveal the clues to the reader/audience.

4. All of the clues and evidence should be made available to the reader/audience.

5. The official police force and their methods are a contrast to the intellect of the detective.

6. There are false clues or 'red herrings' as the plot unfolds to keep the reader guessing.

7. An innocent person is accused before the real culprit is found.

8. There is a gathering of characters at the end to hear the outcome and the solution to the mystery.

KEY CONTEXT (A03)

In 1870 the government voted through an Education Act, which made education compulsory for all children. This meant there were an increasing number of people who could read in Victorian England, from all classes. Conan Doyle's Sherlock Holmes stories were first published in magazines where each chapter would represent one gripping weekly instalment for the Victorian reader. This was a very popular form of entertainment.

TOP TIP (A02)

If you have a favourite TV detective you could think about how many of these conventions are still at work in the form today.

STRUCTURE

CHAPTERS

The Sign of the Four is organised into a sequence of twelve chapters, which work chronologically in terms of time. With the exception of Chapter 12 the chapters are short and pacy. The addition of an enticing hook at the end of each one keeps the reader's interest. The fact that Conan Doyle's work was often published in weekly or monthly parts in magazines helps to explain this structural formula.

THREE-PART PLOT STRUCTURE

The main plot of the novella is organised into a classic three-part plot structure:

- During the early chapters the setting and important characters are established. The characters are drawn into a situation. In *The Sign of the Four* this represents our meeting with Holmes and Watson at Baker Street and Miss Morstan's presentation of her mystery.
- The middle part of the plot introduces a number of obstacles and complications that the characters must work through. This adds tension and excitement for the reader. Holmes presents his theory or hypothesis as to what he thinks is the key to the mystery.
- The plot reaches its climax and ends with a resolution to satisfy the reader. In *The Sign of the Four* the chase along the Thames is the climactic point. Jonathan Small's story explains the mystery in full and proves Holmes's theories to be correct.

NARRATIVE PERSPECTIVE

Essentially the novella is a first-person narrative presented through the character of Dr Watson. He is our main storyteller and operates as a framework narrator. It is Watson's perspective that holds the various elements of the plot together. However, at various points in the plot, we hear from different characters. They take over the narrative and share their own stories. In this way, the novella can be seen to have several narrators, all 'framed' or held together by Watson's overview.

TEXTS WITHIN THE TEXT

Conan Doyle makes interesting use of other texts within the narrative to add variety to the novella. They enable the plot to develop or subtly add to the presentation of characters. The letter that Miss Morstan has received acts as a starting point for the mystery, 'You are a wronged woman ... Do not bring police' (p. 14). This **device** is used by Conan Doyle to introduce the idea of a mystery character and is used to draw Miss Morstan, Holmes and Watson into a different setting so the plot may develop. Newspaper reports are also included in the text, such as on page 72, where we see Jones's inflated sense of importance, 'his powers of minute observation have enabled him to prove conclusively'. Holmes, Watson and the reader know that Jones has proved nothing at this point and the description of his methods is **ironic**. We see a contrast to this on page 84 when Conan Doyle includes the telegram Holmes has sent to Jones: 'Go to Baker street at once'. Here Holmes has assumed control of the investigation and the plot is about to move to its climax.

TOP TIP A02

Watson is our framework narrator. Make a list of all of the other characters in the novella who take over the narrative at various points and tell their own story to help the plot develop. What does each story reveal to the reader that we did not know before? How does each story help Holmes (and the reader) to solve the initial mystery set up by Miss Morstan?

TOP TIP: COMMENTING ON THE EFFECT OF STRUCTURE A02

When thinking about the choices a writer has made in how to structure their story, it is important to question why they made those choices. For example, in this short novella, why would Conan Doyle choose to include a romantic subplot with Watson and Miss Morstan? The main plot has adventure and action; what is added to the novella by the subplot?

The subplot is much gentler and is presented as being more wholesome and innocent. In some ways, it shares the secrecy of the main plot. Watson keeps his feelings hidden for fear of being seen as 'a mere vulgar fortune- seeker' (pp. 53–4). The subplot helps to highlight some of the unpleasant characteristics of those involved in the main plot – their greed, for example, in contrast to Miss Morstan's and Watson's relief at the loss of the treasure. There is a moral factor in that they find love, which is seen as more valuable than money, 'Whoever had lost a treasure, I knew that night that I had gained one' (p. 105).

LANGUAGE

The language of *The Sign of the Four* can be complex, with some words and phrases that a modern reader may not recognise. Conan Doyle uses vivid description in the text to present people and places and to create tension.

LANGUAGE DEVICE: METAPHORS AND SIMILES

What are metaphors and similes?	A metaphor describes one thing as something different, allowing you to make a comparison in your mind's eye. A simile suggests a comparison by using the words 'like' or 'as' to help you see it.
Example	'This Agra treasure intervened like an impassable barrier between us' (p. 54)
Effect	This suggests that Watson views the treasure as an obstacle in the path of his love for Miss Morstan as it would make her rich and therefore socially superior to him.

TOP TIP (A02)

The novella has some references that are difficult to understand, such as to other writers, as well as phrases in French and German. These complexities are not there to baffle the reader, but help to portray Holmes himself as being complex and intellectual.

Conan Doyle uses both metaphor and simile frequently in the novella to create imagery. This was important for his contemporary readership as it gave the stories a visual and almost cinematic feel. The inventive use of imagery adds to the characterful nature of the novella for example when Toby the dog is described as being 'like a connoisseur sniffing the bouquet of a famous vintage' (p. 59).

LANGUAGE DEVICE: PATHETIC FALLACY

What is pathetic fallacy?	Where human emotions are used to describe the natural world and the environment so that they give a sense of the mood or atmosphere in the story.
Example	'Mud-colored clouds drooped sadly over the muddy streets … the dull heavy evening … combined to make me nervous and depressed' (pp. 19–20)
Effect	At this point in the novella, the mystery is still fresh. The reader does not know what to anticipate after the coach journey through London, and neither do the characters. The atmosphere of the evening reflects the mood of the story and the feelings Watson is experiencing.

Conan Doyle's use of pathetic fallacy can add to the suspense and tension of the mystery. By presenting the atmosphere and surroundings as being part of the mystery itself, it can lend the novella a more sinister feel in places. It can help us to empathise with the anxiety that characters such as Watson and Miss Morstan may be feeling as they venture to unknown destinations.

LANGUAGE DEVICE: USE OF DIALOGUE TO CREATE CHARACTER

What is dialogue?	The words that are spoken by the characters in conversation.
Example	'Do you follow all this?' 'Very clearly.' 'Now, what could Jonathan Small do?' (p. 62)
Effect	The dialogue between Holmes and Watson reveals all of the clues that Holmes has gathered. His discussion with Watson is a **device** to keep the reader involved.

The dialogue in the novella gives us the chance to witness the exchanges between characters and to hear their stories. At the point where there is a story to tell about a character – for example, Thaddeus Sholto's account of his father – it is presented through dialogue.

LANGUAGE DEVICE: IRONY

What is irony?	Saying one thing whilst meaning another, perhaps in an understatement or to create humour.
Example	'The prompt and energetic action of the officers of the law shows the great advantage of the presence on such occasions of a single vigorous and masterful mind' (p. 72)
Effect	The extract from the newspaper article could be describing Holmes because the reference to the 'single and vigorous mind' seems to suit him perfectly. The irony here is that this is the report of Athelney Jones's investigation, which was nothing like the way it is described.

The use of irony in the novella helps to highlight the gap between Jones's methods and Holmes's. Conan Doyle is showing the police force to be rather ineffective. However, he also makes fun of himself in Chapter 1. Holmes criticises Watson for writing a 'romance' called *A Study in Scarlet*. In reality this was another story written by Conan Doyle himself.

KEY QUOTATION: THE STRONG ARM OF THE LAW (A02)

Holmes is being ironic when he describes the arrival of the police in mock respectful terms: '"But halloo! Here are the accredited representatives of the law." Heavy steps and the clamour of loud voices were audible from below, and the hall door shut with a loud crash' (p. 47). Conan Doyle shows this when he follows up this line with the description of their clumsy, almost bungling arrival as they barge into the murder scene.

TOP TIP (A02)

Dialogue helps to give more of a picture of a character. For example, the strong **dialect** of Mr Sherman gives the reader clues to class and his manner, 'It hain't got no fangs, so I gives it the run o' the room' (p. 55).

KEY CONTEXT **A03**

Some academics and critics today look back at nineteenth-century works that deal with themes connected to the British Empire. This is called **post-colonial criticism**. They consider, for example, the language used to describe Tonga and Small's Sikh accomplices. Are these the views of the characters in the **novella** or the author himself? Conan Doyle was famous for campaigning for social justice. He was even involved in a campaign to clear the name of an Indian doctor wrongfully accused of a crime.

LANGUAGE DEVICE: SCIENCE AND REASON

What is the language of science and reason?	Words and phrases in the text that are connected to science or scientific thought.
Example	'When I had succeeded in dissolving the hydrocarbon which I was at work at … that always remained as a possible hypothesis' (p. 90)
Effect	Holmes treats the case in the same way he does his chemical experiments. This produces clear thoughts and rational explanations.

Conan Doyle captures the spirit of the time through this choice of language. He makes use of the language of science to give Holmes a superior edge in terms of his knowledge. This gives him the capacity to outsmart his contemporaries – not just the suspects, but the regular police force and his friend Watson – himself a man of science.

TOP TIP **A03**

How might a post-colonial critic respond to the information Small gives us? 'We earned a living at this time by my exhibiting poor Tonga at fairs and other such places as the black cannibal. He would eat raw meat and dance his war-dance; so we always had a hatful of pennies after a day's work' (p. 130). What does this tell us about attitudes at the time? What is implied about the status given to Tonga?

LANGUAGE DEVICE: RACE

What is the language that represents race?	The words and phrases that were used at the time of writing to describe the characters who were not white British.
Example	'It straightened itself into a little black man … with a great, misshapen head and a shock of tangled, dishevelled hair. Holmes had already drawn his revolver, and I whipped out mine at the sight of this savage, distorted creature' (p. 96)
Effect	This is Watson's view when he sees Tonga for the first time. By drawing their guns both Holmes and Watson seem to see Tonga as a wild animal and not as a human being. It suggests they place less value on Tonga's life than they do on Small's, whom they do not shoot.

Much of the language focuses on the native peoples as being, by nature, brutal and uncivilised. This suggests how fearful the Victorians may have been of different races. There is much **irony** in this when we consider the actions of Small, Major Sholto and Captain Morstan, the white representatives of empire.

PROGRESS AND REVISION CHECK

SECTION ONE: CHECK YOUR KNOWLEDGE

1 What does Sherlock Holmes have in common with the fictional detective August Dupin?

2 How did magazines publish stories such as *The Sign of the Four*?

3 Why were more people reading by the late 1800s?

4 What type of structure is the main plot organised into?

5 What type of narrator is Doctor Watson?

6 Name at least two types of text that Conan Doyle uses to add interest to the structure of *The Sign of the Four*.

7 Conan Doyle includes phrases and quotations from which two European languages in the novella?

8 What is the difference between a simile and a metaphor?

9 'The whole place, with its scattered dirt-heaps and ill-grown shrubs, had a blighted, ill-omened look which harmonized with the black tragedy which hung over it' (p. 59): name the language device.

10 Which character uses the language of science and reason the most?

TOP TIP **A01**

Answer these quick questions to test your basic knowledge of the form, structure and language of the novella.

SECTION TWO: CHECK YOUR UNDERSTANDING

Task: How does Conan Doyle make use of letters, newspaper articles and telegrams in *The Sign of the Four*? Think about:

- The different ways they help the plot develop
- How the language of each text is used to create a different effect.

TOP TIP **A01**

This task requires more thought and a slightly longer response. Try to write at least three to four paragraphs.

PROGRESS CHECK

GOOD PROGRESS

I can:

- explain how Conan Doyle uses form, structure and language to develop the action, show relationships and develop ideas. ☐
- use relevant quotations to support the points I make, and make reference to the effect of some language choices. ☐

EXCELLENT PROGRESS

I can:

- analyse in detail Conan Doyle's use of particular forms, structures and language techniques to convey ideas, create characters and evoke mood or setting. ☐
- select from a range of evidence, including apt quotations, to infer the effect of particular language choices and to develop wider interpretations. ☐

UNDERSTANDING THE QUESTION

For your exam, you will be answering an extract-based question and/or a question on the whole of *The Sign of the Four*. Check with your teacher to see what sort of question you are doing. Whatever the task, questions in exams will need **decoding.** This means highlighting and understanding the key words so that the answer you write is relevant.

TOP TIP (A02)

When discussing Conan Doyle's language, make sure you refer to the techniques he uses and, most importantly, the effect of those techniques. Don't just say, 'Conan Doyle uses lots of adjectives and adverbs here'; write, 'Conan Doyle's use of adjectives and adverbs shows/ demonstrates/ conveys the idea that ...'.

BREAK DOWN THE QUESTION

Pick out the **key words** or phrases. For example:

Question: Read the extract from Chapter 12 from 'It lay where he had dropped it' (p. 120, to 'so I just held on and bided my time' (p. 122).

How does Conan Doyle present the treasure and the theme of wealth in **this extract** and in the novella **as a whole**?

What does this tell you?

● Focus on **the treasure** itself and the **attitudes of different characters** towards it at different times. Think about what **wealth** means to **different characters** in the **novella.**
● The word **'present'** tells you that you should focus on the ways Conan Doyle reveals these attitudes, i.e. the techniques he uses.
● The phrases **'this extract'** and **'novella as a whole'** mean you need to **start** with the given **extract** and then **widen your discussion** to the rest of the novella, but stick to the theme **in both**.

PLANNING YOUR ANSWER

It is vital that you generate ideas quickly and plan your answer efficiently when you sit the exam. Stick to your plan and, with a watch at your side, tick off each part as you progress.

STAGE 1: GENERATE IDEAS QUICKLY

Briefly **list your key ideas** based on the question you have **decoded**. For example:

In the **extract**:

● *Small's story reveals the sheer amount of treasure and precious gemstones that made up the loot.*
● *The box of treasure is buried with the body of Achmet; a reminder that the treasure is connected to theft, betrayal and murder.*
● *The thieves all receive lengthy prison sentences where they can't enjoy their wealth. It is of no benefit to them at all.*

In the **novella as a whole**:

- *The treasure is linked to Major Sholto's betrayal and greed.*
- *The wealth the treasure would bring to Miss Morstan might prevent Watson from marrying her.*
- *Small throws the treasure into the Thames and sees it as a curse.*

STAGE 2: JOT DOWN USEFUL QUOTATIONS (OR KEY EVENTS)

For example, from the **extract**, 'When we had feasted our eyes we took them all out and made a list of them' (p. 120).

From the **novella as a whole**: 'Whoever had lost a treasure, I knew that night that I had gained one' (p. 105).

STAGE 3: PLAN FOR PARAGRAPHS

Use paragraphs to plan your answer. For example:

Paragraph	Point
Paragraph 1	**Introduce** the **argument** you wish to make: *In this extract, for the first time, we learn the full extent of the treasure and how it came to be in the hands of Jonathan Small. However, we also see how the treasure has failed to benefit him through his life.*
Paragraph 2	**Your first point**: *The treasure is seen as something tempting to all of the characters involved in plotting to steal it. Their greed is shown when Small tells us how they 'feasted our eyes' as they looked at it.*
Paragraph 3	**Your second point**: *The treasure is hidden with the dead body of the merchant, a sharp reminder that it is connected with murder and betrayal.*
Paragraph 4	**Your third point**: *This betrayal is shown elsewhere in the novella when we learn of Major Sholto's hoarding of the treasure over many years.*
Paragraph 5	**Your fourth point**: *Only Miss Morstan is not greedy for the treasure. There is perhaps a moral message here about what is truly valuable in life, 'Whoever had lost a treasure, I knew that night that I had gained one.'*
	(You may want to add further paragraphs if you have time.)
Conclusion	**Sum up** your argument: *Over the years the treasure has not benefited anyone who has come into contact with it, leading Small to consider it cursed.*

TOP TIP A01

You may not have time to write such a detailed plan in the exam, but this is a good example of how to structure your ideas into paragraphs. Remember to back up your points with evidence from the text, events or quotations.

RESPONDING TO WRITERS' EFFECTS

The two most important assessment objectives are **AO1** and **AO2**. They are about *what* writers do (the choices they make, and the effects these create), *what* your ideas are (your analysis and interpretation) and *how* you write about them (how well you explain your ideas).

ASSESSMENT OBJECTIVE 1   (AO1)

What does it say?	What does it mean?	Dos and don'ts
Read, understand and respond to texts. Students should be able to: ● Maintain a critical style and develop an informed personal response ● Use textual references, including quotations, to support and illustrate interpretations	You must: ● Use some of the literary terms you have learned (correctly!) ● Write in a professional way (not a sloppy, chatty way) ● Show that you have thought for yourself ● Back up your ideas with examples, including quotations	**Don't write …** *Thaddeus Sholto is really ugly. Conan Doyle uses horrible words to describe him.* **Do write …** *Conan Doyle presents Thaddeus Sholto as rather unattractive with his 'pendulous lip' and 'irregular teeth'. However, he is shown to have a kind and thoughtful character, in that he wants to be fair to Miss Morstan. This is in contrast to his twin brother Bartholomew who has a similar appearance but is ….*

IMPROVING YOUR CRITICAL STYLE

Use a variety of words and phrases to show effects: For example:

Conan Doyle *suggests …, conveys…, implies…, presents how …, explores …, demonstrates .., describes how …, shows how …*

I/we (as readers) *infer …, recognise …, understand …, question …, see …, are given …, reflect …*

> For example, look at these two alternative paragraphs by different students about Mary Morstan. Note the difference in the quality of expression.
>
> **Student A:**
>
> *Treats Watson as the writer and is very chatty*
>
> *The point and quotation are repetitive*
>
> Watson says that Mary is really pretty and it's like love at first sight for him. He is really bothered about her when they go to Pondicherry Lodge as he thinks she will be frightened. We know he tries to protect her as he holds her hand, 'Miss Morstan and I stood together and her hand was in mine.' Mary stays back a bit and looks after the housekeeper Mrs Bernstone who is also frightened. In Victorian times women were seen as much weaker than the men, which explains why Conan Doyle did not make them part of the action.
>
> *Very informal*
>
> *Attempts a contextual idea but very simply done*

Student B:

Conan Doyle presents Mary Morstan in a stereotypical way. She is described to us through Watson's eyes, who sees her attractive qualities from his first meeting with her. Watson sees it as 'the most natural thing' that Mary should turn to him for 'comfort and protection' at Pondicherry Lodge. Rather than being part of the action, Mary's role is reduced to taking care of another female character, the housekeeper, Mrs Bernstone. Phrases such as 'soothing effect' and 'womanly comfort' help to portray Mary as perfect in Watson's view and help to show how middle-class women were viewed at the time.

The focus here is on the writer

The supporting quotations are blended into the point

Clearly and formally explained

Precise textual details open up a contextual link

ASSESSMENT OBJECTIVE 2 (A02)

What does it say?	What does it mean?	Dos and don'ts
Analyse the language, form and structure used by the writer to create meanings and effects, using relevant subject terminology where appropriate.	'Analyse' = comment **in detail** on **particular aspects** of the text or language 'Language' = vocabulary, imagery, variety of sentences, dialogue, etc. 'Form' = **how** the story is told (e.g. first-person narrative, letters, newspaper articles, chapter by chapter) 'Structure' = the **order** in which events are revealed, characters appear, or descriptions are presented 'create meaning' = what can we, as readers, **infer** from what the writer tells us? What is **implied** by particular descriptions, or events? 'Subject terminology' = **words** you should use when writing about novellas, such as imagery, setting, etc.	**Don't write ...** *The writing is really descriptive in this bit so you could really imagine how scary Pondicherry Lodge is.* **Do write ...** *Conan Doyle **conveys** a sense of drama and **tension** through the **setting** of Pondicherry Lodge. The use of **pathetic fallacy** in the presentation of the 'desolate grounds' and the Lodge itself surrounded by 'gloom and deathly silence' (p. 36) create a **Gothic** feel to the place.*

IMPLICATIONS, INFERENCES AND INTERPRETATIONS

- The best analysis focuses on specific ideas, events or language and considers what is **implied**.
- This means drawing **inferences**. On the surface, Small's desire to reclaim the treasure after he has served his prison sentence may seem justified, but what about where the treasure belonged in the first place and what does it tell us about the treasure if men were driven to murder for it?
- From the inferences you make across the text as a whole, you can arrive at your own **interpretation** – a sense of the bigger picture, a wider evaluation of a character, relationship or idea.

USING QUOTATIONS

One of the secrets of success in writing exam essays is to use quotations **effectively**. There are five basic principles:

1. Only quote what is most useful.
2. Do not use a quotation that repeats what you have just written.
3. Put quotation marks, e.g. '...', around the quotation.
4. Write the quotation exactly as it appears in the original.
5. Use the quotation so that it fits neatly into your sentence.

EXAM FOCUS: USING QUOTATIONS

Quotations should be used to develop the line of thought in your essay, and to 'zoom in' on key details, such as language choices. The **mid-level example** below shows a clear and effective way of doing this:

> Conan Doyle presents Holmes as being easily bored when he has no work. "My mind," he said, "rebels at stagnation." This suggests to the reader that Holmes is only happy when he has a case to work on which is stimulating for him intellectually.

A point

A quotation

Explanation/effect

However, really **high-level responses** will go further. They will make an even more precise point, support it with an even more appropriate quotation, focus in on particular words or phrases, and explain the effect or what is implied to make a wider point or draw inferences. Here is an example:

> Conan Doyle presents Holmes as being restless and prone to dark moods and depression when faced with the 'dull routine of existence'. Holmes states, 'Give me problems, give me work, give me the most abstruse cryptogram ... and I am in my own proper atmosphere.' The phrase 'proper atmosphere' implies that intellectual activity is a necessity to Holmes and he is unable to function without it. Conan Doyle sets Holmes's superior intelligence apart from other characters making his extraordinary abilities all the more convincing when compared to the regular police force.

Precise point

Apt quotation

Language feature

Explanation/ implication/ effect

Further development/ link

SPELLING, PUNCTUATION AND GRAMMAR

SPELLING

Remember to spell correctly the **author's** name, the names of all the **characters**, and the names of **places**.

Practise the spellings of key literature terms you might use when writing about the text such as: ironic, Gothic, simile, metaphor, imagery, protagonist, narrator, character, theme, pathetic fallacy, etc.

PUNCTUATION

Remember:

- Use **full stops and commas in sentences accurately to make clear points**. Don't write long, rambling sentences that don't make sense; equally, avoid using a lot of short, repetitive ones. Write in a fluent way, using linking words and phrases, and use **inverted commas** for **quotations**:

Don't write	Do write
Watson is really upset with Holmes and thinks he's unworthy where he gives him his brother's watch to analyse and Holmes tells him every detail about it without thinking Watson may be upset by some of the things he deduces.	*When analysing the pocket watch, Holmes is rather insensitive. He does not consider that he is describing Watson's brother. Watson finds some of Holmes's analysis upsetting and concludes, 'This is unworthy of you, Holmes.'*

GRAMMAR

When you are writing about the text, make sure you:

- Use the **present tense** for discussing what the writer does, e.g. *Conan Doyle shows the reader how and why Major Sholto betrays Morstan and Small to keep the treasure for himself.*
- Vary character names with **pronouns** (he/her) and use references back to make your writing flow.

Don't write	Do write
Despite the fact that Tonga felt he had assisted Small by killing Sholto, Tonga was beaten by his 'master'. Tonga was described in terms showing racial prejudice throughout the novella and was brutally shot as the chase reaches its climax.	*Despite the fact that Tonga feels he has assisted Small by killing Sholto, his 'master' beats him. Throughout the novella Tonga is described in terms showing racial prejudice and he is brutally shot as the chase reaches its climax.*

TOP TIP

Spelling, punctuation and grammar are not assessed by AQA in relation to *The Sign of the Four*. However, it is important to ensure that you write accurately and clearly, in order to get your points across to the examiner in the best possible way.

TOP TIP

Enliven your essay by varying the way your sentences begin. For example, *Thaddeus Sholto is Athelney Jones's prime suspect after he has made a brief examination of the murder scene, just as Sholto feared he would be.* This can also be written as, *After making a brief examination of the murder scene, Jones arrests Bartholomews's twin as his prime suspect, just as Thaddeus Sholto had feared.*

ANNOTATED SAMPLE ANSWERS

This section provides three sample reponses, one at a **mid** level, one at a **good** level, and one at a **very high** level.

> **Question:** Read from 'My mind ... rebels at stagnation' (p. 2) to 'by which I succeed in unraveling it' (p. 3). How does Conan Doyle present Sherlock Holmes as unique
>
> • in this extract
> • in the novella as a whole?

SAMPLE ANSWER 1

Sherlock Holmes seems very unique to us because he wants to do work which is difficult and problematic, 'Give me problems, give me work ...'. He likes a challenge and he says he gets bored very easily otherwise.

He is also unique in that he has invented his own profession and even he thinks he is one of a kind, 'The only unofficial consulting detective'. This suggests it was very unusual at the time for someone to work in the way that Holmes does.

AC Beginning to consider some implications and using supporting quotations

It is also unusual to not want any reward or recognition for what you do but Holmes says that, 'The work itself, the pleasure of finding a field for my peculiar powers, is my highest reward.' This suggests that it is solving the cases that is the main reward for Holmes, like a kind of personal challenge. The word 'peculiar' suggests that Holmes himself thinks he is quite unique.

A01 More interpretation

AC Reference to language

However, Holmes is also quite critical. When he is talking to Watson he says, 'I cannot congratulate you on it.' This suggests he is not happy with the way Watson has presented one of his cases in his story.

A01 Consideration of alternative ideas

In other places in the novella, we know Holmes is critical of others too. For example when he is talking about the police and Athelney Jones. This suggests he does not have a high opinion of them. He is not unkind though as he says, 'He is not a bad fellow ...' about Jones.

A01 A good choice of quotation

A01 A clearly expressed link

We find out more in the novella about his methods of work. He tends to use analysis and logic to solve cases like a puzzle. He also uses close examination and takes a scientific approach. We see this in the way he examines the crime scene at Pondicherry Lodge. The nineteenth century was a time when scientific knowledge expanded rapidly and Holmes uses it to his advantage.

A03 Touches on context

02 A little more consideration of language

Holmes is presented as being clever and we know this when Conan Doyle describes him using phrases like, 'extraordinary concentration' and 'hawk-like features'. Watson also gives his view of Holmes and tells us, 'Holmes alone could rise superior to petty influences.' This suggests ordinary things do not distract him.

It seems that Holmes is very knowledgeable, he has a good memory and many skills such as we see when he thinks about past cases, refers to his books and climbs on the roof to gather more evidence. He uses all of his skills in his work, and he is also very inventive in his methods. For example he wears a disguise when he needs to find the Aurora, and he uses his many contacts and his reputation to gather clues as the novella develops.

A01 Shows some detailed knowledge of the text using textual references rather than direct quotation

01 Attempts a useful conclusion

Even though it says in the extract that 'My name figures in no newspaper' he is clearly known by many people in London by his reputation as a unique, successful and clever detective.

MID LEVEL

Comment

Good points are made about the extract and relevant points are made about Holmes in other parts of the novella. Relevant quotations are provided and there are a number of interpretations made. There are some references to Conan Doyle's use of language. Context is touched on briefly.

For a Good level:

- Develop a more fluent writing style.
- Make greater reference to the effects of language or structure and aim for more confident use of subject terminology.
- Provide more detailed explanations to show deeper understanding.
- Conclude the argument more confidently.

SAMPLE ANSWER 2

Sherlock Holmes is unique in the fact he has invented his own profession as 'The only unofficial consulting detective', suggesting he likes to do things in his own way and without having to answer to others.

A confident interpretation to begin the argument — AO

He seems critical of the way other detectives work and does not think highly of them or their methods, which he may see as lacking in skill. We see this in the extract when he says the others are 'out of their depths', but later in the novella when we are able to contrast Holmes's methods with Jones's at Pondicherry Lodge.

Uses both direct quotation and textual reference to support a key point — AO

AO1 — A well-chosen quotation developing a thoughtful point

Holmes can even be critical of his own closest friend and is very honest with Watson about his feelings about his writing, 'I glanced over it', suggesting it was not worth a closer look. We know that at other times this hurts Watson's feelings, for example when Holmes is insensitive about Watson's brother after examining his watch. This suggests Holmes does not like to compromise in any way, which is shown in his attitude to his work.

A well-expressed link, with evidence — AO

AO2 — Some focus on language and sentence forms with comment on effect

Holmes enjoys the challenge of difficult cases and views all of his work as a way of exercising his mental ability. He makes bold statements such as 'I crave for mental exaltation.' However, both Watson and Mrs Hudson worry about him in Chapter 8 and he is described using adjectives such as 'dejected' and 'morose'. This implies his need for difficult work has a darker side in that when Holmes is bored he becomes very depressed.

In 'The Sign of the Four', Holmes pieces together the mystery almost exactly right after examining the crime scene closely. He is presented using animal imagery as he examines Pondicherry Lodge with, 'beady eyes ... like those of a bird', 'swift, silent and furtive ... like a trained blood hound' as though he is working instinctively. However, he is working much more scientifically and forensically and his approach helps to show the great scientific strides that were made in the nineteenth century and the spirit of change. It is he who works out the connection with the one legged man, he deduces that this has to be Small and he works out he has an accomplice with small bare feet. None of this occurs to Jones who does not examine things with Holmes's unique approach, 'I will make you a free present of the name and description of one of the two people who were in this room last night.'

Further focus on language features and their effects — AC

AO3 — Considers context in relation to character

Another very well-chosen quotation — AC

01

Uses detailed knowledge of the text to make a further interpretation

At other points in the novella Holmes quotes other writers in French and German, he plays the violin, we learn he can wrestle and climb. He is not just an intellectual but has many skills. He uses all of them inventively too – such as when he disguises himself as an old sailor to gain the trust of the people in the boatyards to find the 'Aurora'.

01

A confident concluding point, with an apt quotation

Holmes has a reputation in London. He is recommended to Miss Morstan by a previous client. McMurdo knows him by reputation; Toby's owner is happy to help him; he is able to charm a band of street urchins to help him. Even Jones has to conclude that, 'He's a man who is not to be beat', allowing the reader to see him as an extraordinary character with extraordinary abilities.

GOOD LEVEL

Comment

There is plenty of interpretation of the text here and points are well supported by relevant and, in places, well chosen evidence. There is analysis of language and effects are considered. There is an attempt to comment on context which could be developed further. The essay is well expressed, controlled and organised.

For a Very High level:

- Provide a more sustained analysis of the text and ideas.
- Develop a coherent overall argument, expressed more fluently and elegantly.
- Make more links between close analysis and wider themes, effects of language, etc.
- Demonstrate more of a sense of the writer at work.

SAMPLE ANSWER 3

Holmes is presented to us as a complex and unique character. Within the extract he makes almost a plea, 'Give me the most abstruse cryptogram or the most intricate analysis.' This suggests that work, which provides 'mental exaltation' is a basic need for a man like Holmes. In the opening to the novella, we have just witnessed Watson's concern for Holmes's drug taking which, although disturbing to a modern reader, suggests that Holmes is willing to experiment on his own mind. He seems to view everything he does scientifically and as an intellectual exercise. 'Its secondary action is a matter of small moment', he concludes about the cocaine.

A0 Uses a contextual aspect to support the initial interpretation

Holmes has invented his own profession as 'the only unofficial consulting detective'. Perhaps this implies he finds it difficult to cope with any other methodology apart from his own. It could also suggest a little arrogance on his part, something Watson considers when he says he is 'irritated by the egotism' of his colleague.

A01 Considers alternative interpretations with apt, embedded quotations

Holmes operates rationally and logically, pinpointing evidence with close examination. 'You have an extraordinary gift for minutiae', Watson remarks. Yet there is also evidence that he works instinctively too. This is most closely seen in the language used to describe Holmes at the crime scene where he is compared to a bird with his 'beady eyes' and a bloodhound, 'picking out a scent'. The triplet, 'swift, silent and furtive', describes his method but also makes an interesting contrast. This language might also describe how a criminal operates and Watson even considers 'what a terrible criminal' Holmes might have made. It seems that Holmes can anticipate the actions and thought processes of the suspects. This is certainly the case when he explores the crime scene at Pondicherry Lodge.

AC Another precise quotation leading into an alternative interpretation

A02 Close analysis of language with developed comment leading to further inference

Though Jones dismisses him as a 'theorist' it is Holmes who gathers enough clues to allow him to present an almost complete hypothesis almost immediately. His mind seems to work at a faster pace than the others, leading to his impatience and frustration with others. He chides Watson for this, 'My dear Watson, try a little analysis yourself.' In the extract we see how Holmes is dismissive of the police force

01 Complex, well-constructed idea

and considers them to be 'out of their depths'. However, he later criticises Jones's swift pace and 'immense display of energy' with gentle humour when he tells Watson Jones has arrested everyone at Pondicherry Lodge, which adds another layer of interest and complexity to Holmes's character.

A01 Precise quotations help to maintain the argument

Though connected with logic, Conan Doyle presents his detective as inventive and creative in his approaches too: his use of disguise, his contacts, his methods of questioning are just some examples. Holmes's knowledge and memory seem extensive. He has unusual skills – he is athletic, a linguist, musical. Conan Doyle's character is out of the ordinary and able to rise above the mundane.

A02 Considers the writer's effects

However, Conan Doyle also presents Holmes as representing aspects of characters associated with the Gothic genre, in both the darker elements of his nature, and in the way duality is reflected through his relationship with Watson. This shows that however original Holmes appears, the author was drawing on the ideas of his time to create his detective.

A03 Uses contextual knowledge to add a different angle

01 Structures the argument to return to the extract to help create a cohesive conclusion

Holmes is accomplished and skilled but he does have flaws. The extract has shown Holmes to be paralysed by boredom and desperate for stimulation. When the pace of the novella slows down as the search for the 'Aurora' becomes fruitless, Holmes becomes 'morose' and 'dejected'. His periods of dark depression suggest he is a man who was not born for 'the dull routine of existence'. In this way, perhaps Watson is right to conclude this unique individual is 'a calculating machine!'

A01 Fluently woven-in quotations create the confident conclusion

VERY HIGH LEVEL

Comment

The convincing argument is structured and expressed confidently, using some very precise references and quotations. Strong, confident textual knowledge is evident and contextual considerations are used to assist and develop the argument. The author's choices of language are explored in detailed with effects commented on confidently and perceptively. The writing style is elegant and fluent, with cohesive and coherent links made between the paragraphs to help construct a compelling argument.

PRACTICE TASK

Write a full-length response to this exam-style question and then use the **Mark scheme** on page 80 to assess your own response.

> Read from 'We followed the Indian' (p. 23) to 'the modern French school' (p. 26). How does Conan Doyle present Thaddeus Sholto as an interesting and eccentric character
>
> - in this extract
> - in the novella as a whole?

TOP TIP (A01)

You can use the General Skills section of the **Mark scheme** on page 80 to remind you of the key criteria you'll need to cover.

Remember:

- Plan quickly and efficiently by using key words from the question.
- Write equally about the extract and the rest of the novella.
- Focus on the techniques Conan Doyle uses and the effect of these on the reader.
- Support your ideas with relevant evidence, including quotations.

FURTHER QUESTIONS

1 Read from 'She was seated by the open window' (p. 102) to 'I had gained one' (p. 105). How does Conan Doyle present the theme of love and friendship

- in this extract
- in the novella as a whole?

2 Read from 'It was a September evening' (p. 19) to 'a third-rate suburban dwelling-house' (p. 22). How does Conan Doyle make use of London as a setting for *The Sign of the Four*

- in this extract
- in the novella as a whole?

3 Read from '"Dear little chap!" said Holmes, strategically' (p. 67) to 'you are very likely to get what you want' (p. 69). How does Conan Doyle present issues of class and status

- in this extract
- in the novella as a whole?

LITERARY TERMS

adjective	a word used to describe a noun, e.g. 'a *starry* night', 'a *happy* sight'
anticlimax	a part of the narrative where the tension melts or is let down purposely
atmosphere	the mood of a setting or situation
chronological	a style of narrative where the events are ordered in time sequence
climax	the part of a narrative with the greatest emotional tension
device	a technique used by an author for a specific effect
dialect	vocabulary and/or grammar which is specific to a particular community, area or region
dialogue	the words that are spoken by characters in conversation
duality	describes how an aspect of a work of fiction, such as a character, location or theme, can represent two opposing sides, such as good and evil, light and dark
fable	a short story that contains a moral
genre	a type of literature, e.g. poetry, drama, biography, fiction, or style of literature, e.g. Gothic or romance
Gothic	literature that contains supernatural, unexplained and weird events in order to provoke either terror or horror in the reader with nightmarish images
imagery	creating a word picture; common forms are metaphors and similes
imperative	a verb used to give orders or instructions
irony	saying one thing while meaning another, often through understatement, concealment or indirect statement; dramatic irony is when the audience or reader is aware of something the character is not
metaphor	a figure of speech in which something, someone or an action is described as something else in order to imply a resemblance, e.g. Watson calling Holmes a 'calculating machine'
narrative	a story or account of events, real or imagined; a first-person narrative is a story told from the point of view of the central character, using 'I'
narrator	the voice telling the story or relating a sequence of events; a framework narrator holds the plot together in a work of fiction, where other characters tell their stories at various points
noun phrase	a short phrase which includes a noun and an adjective or adjectives to describe it, e.g. 'the dark night'
novella	a story that is longer than a short story but not quite long enough to be considered a novel
pathetic fallacy	when setting (often the weather) reflects the mood of a character or scene
pivotal moment	a crucial or climactic moment in the plot of a story where a turning point happens and we move towards a resolution
post-colonial criticism	explores texts that were written in the past and re-examines them from a modern perspective, questioning their attitudes to race and other cultures
protagonist	the central character of a novel or narrative
resolution	the ending of a work of fiction where all questions are answered and all plotlines reach their conclusion
setting	the place or environment where the events in a story are set, sometimes used symbolically or to create a mood or reflect a character's inner feelings
simile	a figure of speech using 'like' or 'as' to make a comparison
standard English	the dialect of English that is used in formal speech and writing
subplot	a second storyline within a work of fiction that happens alongside the main plot
symbolise	to use an image to mean or represent something else, often an idea or emotion

CHECKPOINT ANSWERS

1 Gregson, Lestrade, Athelney Jones

2 He is just an army surgeon with an injured leg; he is not wealthy

3 'She must have been more than woman if she did not feel some uneasiness at the strange enterprise upon which we were embarking, yet her self-control was perfect' (p. 18); 'Miss Morstan's demeanor was as resolute and collected as ever' (p. 21)

4 He asks him to check the mitral valve of his heart

5 McMurdo, who knew Holmes as he had fought him in a boxing match, and Mrs Bernstone, the housekeeper

6 Streatham, Brixton, Camberwell, the Oval, Kennington Lane, Bond Street, Miles Street, Knight's Place, Nine Elms

7 The launch is called the *Aurora*; she is small and trim; she is freshly painted black with two red streaks; her funnel is black with a white band

8 Westminster Stairs at 7 p.m.

9 To a ship called the *Esmerelda*, which was at Gravesend and was sailing for the Brazils

10 Abdullah Khan, Mahomet Singh, Dost Akbar

PROGRESS AND REVISION CHECK ANSWERS

PART TWO, PAGES 34–5

SECTION ONE

1. A watch

2. Mrs Hudson

3. The Langham Hotel, London

4. 7 July

5. A coachman, Williams

6. A glass of Chianti

7. He fears no one will believe he did not murder him as even his own servant doesn't

8. 11 o'clock

9. Bartholomew Sholto

10. So that his footprints will not add any complications to the investigation

11. A long, black, poisoned thorn

12. To Sherman's shop at No. 3 Pinchin Lane

13. Half spaniel, half lurcher; brown and white

14. He was still a convict and could not get away

15. Mordecai Smith's

16. Wiggins

17. He paces his room, then stays up to work on a chemical experiment

18. Fifteen

19. He feels he can now tell Miss Morstan that he loves her

20. He was a ruined man, having lost everything when gambling

SECTION TWO

Task 1: Possible Plan

- Holmes is an unusual character who has invented his own profession as a detective. 'I am the last and highest court of appeal in detection' (p. 3).

- He needs to be constantly working on a problem and is restless and bored when he is not doing so. '"My mind," he said, "rebels at stagnation"' (p. 2).

- Holmes and Watson are presented as good friends with a trusting relationship, though Watson seems a little wary of Holmes: 'His great powers, his masterly manner, and the experience which I had had of his many extraordinary qualities, all made me diffident and backward in crossing him' (p. 1).

- Watson praises Holmes's fine skills as a detective but considers him to be rather insensitive to human feelings at times: '"This is unworthy of you Holmes," I said' (p. 8).

Task 2: Possible Plan

- The characters arrive at Pondicherry Lodge in the dark and it is described as a gloomy mysterious, unwelcoming place: 'The vast size of the building, with its gloom and its deathly silence, struck a chill to the heart' (p. 36).

- The idea of the grounds dug over for the treasure links it with the mystery so far: 'Inside, a gravel path wound through desolate grounds' (p. 36).

- Tension is created through the locked room and Holmes's discovery of Bartholomew Sholto's murdered body: '"There is something devilish in this, Watson," said he, more moved than I had ever before seen him' (p. 39).

- There is more excitement created as the strange circumstances of the murder are revealed and we discover the treasure is missing once again: 'By the table, in a wooden arm-chair, the master of the house was seated all in a heap, with his head sunk upon his left shoulder, and that ghastly, inscrutable smile upon his face' (p. 40).

PART THREE, PAGE 45

SECTION ONE

1   Mrs Bernstone

2   Major Sholto

3   Bartholomew

4   McMurdo the prizefighter

5   Mr Sherman

6   Athelney Jones (p. 70)

7   Wiggins

8   Dost Akbar, Abdullah Khan, Mahomet Singh

9   Mordecai Smith

10 Tonga (p. 128)

SECTION TWO

Possible Plan

- Holmes is presented as rational, thoughtful and logical as he weighs up the evidence. 'He whipped out his lens and a tape measure, and hurried about the room on his knees, measuring, comparing, examining, with his long thin nose only a few inches from the planks, and his beady eyes gleaming and deep-set like those of a bird' (p. 46).

- He is presented as a precise and measured man in contrast to the regular police force. 'Heavy steps and the clamor of loud voices were audible from below, and the hall door shut with a loud crash' (p. 47).

- Watson questions him but seems in awe of his skills and the speed at which he deduces the facts. 'I marvel at the means by which you obtain your results in this case … How, for example, could you describe with such confidence the wooden-legged man?' (p. 60).

- Watson is amazed at the effect Holmes has on other people and how his reputation has spread among such a variety of people in London. '"Mr. Sherlock Holmes–" I began, but the words had a most magical effect' (p. 55).

PART FOUR, PAGE 55

SECTION ONE

1   The theft of the Agra treasure (twice) and the murder of the convict guard

2   Holmes in Chapter 12

3   It would give Mary financial independence

4   Thaddeus and Bartholomew Sholto

5   Charles Darwin in his work *On the Origin of Species*

6   The Indian Mutiny 1857

7   The Andaman islanders (p. 71)

8   The Jack the Ripper murders

9   Pondicherry Lodge

10 Agra

SECTION TWO

Possible Plan

- Wealth is presented negatively in the novella and seems to be connected with greed and betrayal, such as that shown by Major Sholto, 'The cursed greed which has been my besetting sin through life has withheld from her the treasure, half at least of which should have been hers' (p. 28).

- To Jonathan Small the treasure is rightfully his after his long imprisonment, 'It is my treasure; and if I can't have the loot I'll take darned good care that no one else does' (p. 107).

- The treasure could be seen to represent how India was plundered by the British, 'We only ask you to do that which your countrymen come to this land for. We ask you to be rich' (p. 114).

- However, the treasure is also seen as a curse and an impediment to Watson's happiness, 'Because this treasure, these riches, sealed my lips. Now that they are gone I can tell you how I love you' (p. 105).

PART FIVE, PAGE 61

Possible Plan

- It is the letter Miss Morstan has received that is the starting point for the case, 'Be at the third pillar from the left outside the Lyceum Theatre to-night at seven o'clock. If you are distrustful, bring two friends. You are a wronged woman, and shall have justice' (p. 14).

- The advertisement in the newspaper led to the mailing of the pearls. This introduces the idea of the treasure into the plot, 'an advertisement appeared in the Times asking for the address of Miss Mary Morstan' (p. 13).

- The newspaper articles help to contrast Holmes with Jones, '"Here it is," said he, laughing, and pointing to an open newspaper. "The energetic Jones and the ubiquitous reporter have fixed it up between them"' (p. 71).

- The telegram summoning Jones helps us to realise that Holmes has made progress and we anticipate an exciting conclusion. 'I am close on the track of the Sholto gang. You can come with us to-night if you want to be in at the finish' (p. 84).

SECTION ONE

1 Both are eccentric, logical, use reasoning, make close observations to solve crimes

2 In weekly or monthly instalments

3 The Education Act of 1870 made it compulsory for children to attend school, leading to more people reading

4 A three-part plot structure

5 Framework narrator

6 Letter, newspaper article, telegram

7 French and German

8 A simile makes a comparison between two things, a metaphor states a thing is something else

9 Pathetic fallacy

10 Sherlock Holmes

MARK SCHEME

POINTS YOU COULD HAVE MADE

In the extract:

- Thaddeus Sholto is a strange figure with a 'bald, shining scalp' and 'irregular teeth' (p. 23).
- Though tactless, he does not want to cheat Miss Morstan: 'it would have been bad taste to have treated a young lady in so scurvy a fashion' (p. 31).
- He is presented as eccentric in his tastes and dress sense and his room reflects his unusual personality (see p. 26).

In the rest of the novella:

- Sholto creates the mystery by sending the pearls to Miss Morstan and the anonymous letter. '"It was a kindly thought," said our companion, earnestly' (p. 31).
- We wonder what he and his brother may be covering up: 'Nothing would annoy Brother Bartholomew more than any publicity' (p. 25).
- His response to his brother's death adds interest: 'He was ... the very picture of terror, wringing his hands and moaning to himself' (p. 41).

GENERAL SKILLS

Make a judgement about your level based on the points you made (above) and the skills you showed.

Level	Key elements	Writing skills	Tick your level
Very high	**Very well-structured answer which gives a rounded and convincing viewpoint.** You use very detailed analysis of the writer's methods and effects on the reader, using precise references which are fluently woven into what you say. You draw inferences, consider more than one perspective or angle, including the context where relevant, and make interpretations about the text as a whole.	You spell and punctuate with consistent accuracy, and use a very wide range of vocabulary and sentence structures to achieve effective control of meaning.	
Good to High	**A thoughtful, detailed response with well-chosen references.** At the top end, you address all aspects of the task in a clearly expressed way, and examine key aspects in detail. You consider implications and different interpretations or ideas; at the top end, you do this fairly regularly and with some confidence.	You spell and punctuate with considerable accuracy, and use a considerable range of vocabulary and sentence structures to achieve general control of meaning.	
Mid	**A consistent response with clear understanding of the main ideas shown.** You use a range of references to support your ideas and your viewpoint is logical and easy to follow. Some comment on writers' effects, though more needed.	You spell and punctuate with reasonable accuracy, and use a reasonable range of vocabulary and sentence structures.	
Lower	**Some relevant ideas but an inconsistent and simple response in places.** You show you understand the task and you make some points to support what you say, but the evidence is not always well chosen. Your analysis is basic and you do not comment in detail on the writer's methods.	Your spelling and punctuation is inconsistent and your vocabulary and sentence structures are both limited. This can make your meaning unclear.	